The Hebrew Book of Enoch

Mystical Visions and Divine Secrets

A Modern Translation

Adapted for the Contemporary Reader

Rabbi Ishmael
(Jewish Mysticism)

Translated by Tim Zengerink

Table Of Contents

Preface - Message to the Reader

What If You Could Help Rebuild the Greatest Library in Human History?

Thousands of years ago, the Library of Alexandria stood as the crown jewel of human achievement — a sanctuary where the collected wisdom of every known civilization was gathered, preserved, and shared freely.

And then, it was lost.

Through fire, conquest, and the slow erosion of time, humanity lost not just books — but ideas, dreams, discoveries, and stories that could have changed the world forever.

Today, the Library of Alexandria lives again — and you are invited to be a part of its restoration.

Our mission is simple yet profound:

To rebuild the greatest library the world has ever known, and to translate all timeless works into every language and dialect, so that no seeker of knowledge is ever left behind again.

By joining our movement to rebuild the modern Library of Alexandria, you become part of an unprecedented mission:

- **Unlimited Access to the Greatest Audiobooks & eBooks Ever Written:**

  Instantly explore thousands of legendary works—Plato, Shakespeare, Jane Austen, Leo Tolstoy, and countless more. All instantly available to read or listen, placing a complete literary universe at your fingertips.

- **Beautiful Paperback & Deluxe Editions at Printing Cost**

  Own any title as an elegant paperback, deluxe hardcover, or stunning collectible boxset—offered to you at true printing cost, delivered straight to your door. Build your personal Library of Alexandria, crafted for beauty, built for durability, and worthy of proud display.

- **Fresh Translations for Modern Readers—in Every Language & Dialect**

  Enjoy timeless masterpieces reimagined in clear, contemporary language—no more outdated phrases or obscure references. Alongside the original versions, we're tirelessly translating these classics into every language and dialect imaginable, ensuring accessibility and understanding across cultures and generations.

- **Join a Global Renaissance of Literature & Knowledge**

  You directly support expanding our library, publishing deluxe editions at true cost, translating works into all global languages, and bringing humanity's greatest stories to people everywhere. By joining today, you're not just preserving a legacy of masterpieces; you set in motion a powerful wave of literary accessibility.

Become a Torchbearer of Knowledge.

Join us for free now at **LibraryofAlexandria.com**

Together, we will ensure that the light of human wisdom never fades again.

With gratitude and a shared love of knowledge,

The Modern Library of Alexandria Team

Visit:

www.libraryofalexandria.com

Or scan the code below:

Introduction

Rabbi Ishmael's Ascent and the Revelation of Hidden Worlds

Among the sacred and mysterious writings of Jewish mysticism, few are as awe-inspiring and enigmatic as The Hebrew Book of Enoch, also known as 3 Enoch. Attributed to Rabbi Ishmael, a revered second-century Tanna and high priest, this remarkable text transports the reader into the vast and ordered structure of the heavens. Through the medium of a visionary ascent, Rabbi Ishmael is granted access to the celestial realm and invited to witness the hidden operations of the divine world. What he sees, hears, and records forms the foundation for much of later Jewish mystical thought, particularly in the traditions of Hekhalot and Merkabah mysticism. Here, heaven is not a distant abstraction, but a vivid and ordered reality filled with fiery angels, luminous thrones, divine palaces, and exalted hierarchies of power. And at the center of it all is the glory of the Most High—radiant, immeasurable, and surrounded by hosts that tremble in worship.

The Hebrew Book of Enoch is not merely a narrative of ascent; it is a theological and mystical revelation of the universe as a living structure governed by justice, holiness, and divine presence. In this sacred account, Rabbi Ishmael does not ascend by his own merit or curiosity. He is summoned—called upward into the heavens as part of a divine invitation to see what lies behind the veil of human perception. He is accompanied by the angel Metatron, who becomes his guide and interpreter of the mysteries. What follows is a detailed journey through the heavenly palaces (hekhalot), filled with both majestic vision and trembling fear. Every corner of the heavens is guarded, every revelation comes with a warning, and every truth is meant to awaken awe. This is a realm where angels are assigned to record every human action, where the fate of souls is determined, and where the names of God, too sacred to be spoken aloud, radiate unending light.

What distinguishes 3 Enoch from other apocalyptic texts is its clear focus on the transformation of the visionary himself. Rabbi Ishmael is not just a witness— he is being initiated into the mysteries. He is gradually prepared, purified, and elevated in understanding, until he is able to grasp—even if only partially—the workings of the divine court. Central to this experience is his encounter with Metatron, the exalted angel who was once Enoch, the seventh patriarch from Adam, now transformed into the lesser Yahweh and granted extraordinary authority in the heavenly realms. Through this encounter, 3 Enoch connects the earlier Enochic traditions found in 1 Enoch and 2 Enoch with the later mystical explorations of God's celestial palace. It reveals how an earthly man, through righteousness and divine favor, can be exalted to near-angelic status, becoming a bridge between heaven and earth.

This notion of transformation is at the heart of the text's mystical teaching. The Hebrew Book of Enoch is not content to simply describe what is seen in heaven—it also reveals the conditions of access. Only those who are purified, obedient, and spiritually awakened may ascend. The deeper mysteries are not given lightly. They are guarded by angels with flaming swords, protected by heavenly seals, and only disclosed to those who approach with fear and reverence. This reflects a key principle of Jewish mysticism: that true knowledge of God is not intellectual alone, but experiential, and it requires the total preparation of the soul. Through Rabbi Ishmael's journey, the reader is invited to consider their own readiness—spiritually, ethically, and emotionally—to receive divine wisdom.

The Architecture of the Divine and the Mystical Worldview

The cosmology presented in The Hebrew Book of Enoch is vast, intricate, and filled with symbolic meaning. It envisions the universe as a structured reality layered with heavenly realms, each one populated by specific orders of angels, ruled by divine laws, and suffused with sacred power. Every palace Rabbi Ishmael visits has its own function: some are places of worship, others of judgment, others of teaching, or recording. The beings who inhabit these realms are not metaphorical—they are fully real within the symbolic logic of the mystical worldview. They act, speak, record, guard, and praise. Each of their movements reflects the will of God and contributes to the orchestration of the cosmos. In this vision, the universe is not mechanical but alive—dynamic with spirit, intention, and energy flowing from the Holy One.

At the center of this system is the Divine Throne and the celestial court, where God is surrounded by myriads of angels, each fulfilling a role in the administration of justice, mercy, and praise. Rabbi Ishmael learns how the prayers of Israel rise through the heavens, how judgment is issued upon the deeds of men, how the names of the righteous are recorded in heavenly books, and how even the most hidden sins are revealed before the throne of glory. He learns the names of angels that govern the stars, the winds, the times, and the seasons. He observes the heavenly scribes at work and hears the proclamations of divine will. But above all, he learns that creation is governed not by randomness or chaos, but by a moral and spiritual order established by God before the foundations of the world.

This understanding is inseparable from the text's ethical teachings. 3 Enoch is not a speculative work meant only to dazzle the imagination—it is a call to righteousness. Through the awe-inspiring visions, the reader is reminded of the seriousness of life, the consequences of sin, and the importance of aligning oneself with the divine will. The heavens reflect back to the earth the reality of God's sovereignty, and the text makes it clear that the lives of human beings are intimately bound up with the activity of heaven. There is no disconnect between spiritual experience and ethical living. To draw near to the mysteries of God is to be drawn deeper into holiness, responsibility, and reverence.

The role of Metatron is especially central to this vision. Once a human being—Enoch—he now stands as the highest of angels, a prince among the heavenly host, second only to God. His transformation reveals that humanity has a spiritual destiny beyond what can be seen or imagined. Metatron embodies the potential of the righteous soul—what it can become when it fully aligns with divine will. He is both guardian and guide, showing Rabbi Ishmael the heavenly paths and reminding him of the weight of the revelations he receives. Through Metatron, the text unites apocalyptic vision with mystical ascent, showing that knowledge of the divine is not merely observed but embodied.

Engaging the Text as a Mystical Journey

Reading The Hebrew Book of Enoch is unlike reading any ordinary religious or historical text. It demands not only intellectual attention but spiritual openness. This is a work meant to be contemplated, not merely analyzed. Its language is symbolic, filled with layers of meaning that unfold gradually through reflection and study. Its images—of fire, light, thrones, seals, angelic names— are not meant to be taken as literal geography but as revelations of the inner structure of spiritual reality. The heavens described are not only external places but also inward states of consciousness and levels of divine awareness. Each ascent is a step toward greater union with the holy.

This modern translation has been carefully prepared to help readers access the richness of the original without being burdened by its archaic forms. Every sentence has been translated line-by-line with attention to clarity, rhythm, and reverence, ensuring the experience remains faithful to the sacred atmosphere of the text while being fully accessible to contemporary readers. Great care has been taken not to lose the poetic and mystical tone that makes this book so extraordinary. The result is a version that retains the power of the original while speaking directly to the spiritual seeker today.

As you enter the pages of The Hebrew Book of Enoch, let yourself be drawn into its rhythm and intensity. Imagine Rabbi Ishmael's trembling before the divine court. Listen to the voices of the angels. Picture the radiance of the throne. Reflect on the balance of justice and mercy that governs the universe. Ask yourself: What does it mean to be righteous? What is my place in the divine order? What might I be shown, if I, too, were called to ascend?

Whether you approach this book as a student of mysticism, a person of faith, or simply someone curious about the deep spiritual traditions of the past, you will find in these pages a mirror to your own longing for truth. This is not a story to be consumed, but a mystery to be entered. In Rabbi Ishmael's ascent, you may find your own spiritual questions answered—or awakened. In the vast structure of the heavens, you may discover not only the secrets of the divine, but also the path toward your own transformation. Let this sacred vision be your guide.

Chapter I

Rabbi Ishmael describes his journey into the heavens, where he saw the divine vision of the Merkaba, God's heavenly chariot. As he passed through each level, each one more incredible than the last, he finally reached the entrance to the seventh and highest realm. There, he stood in prayer before the Holy One, looking up at the brilliant light above. In his heart, he called upon the merit of Aaron, the son of Amram—a man known for spreading peace and kindness—who had been given the honor of priesthood directly by God on Mount Sinai.

Rabbi Ishmael prayed with deep emotion, asking that Aaron's righteousness protect him from Qafsiel, the ruling angel, and the other powerful beings guarding the entrance, so they would not harm him or stop him from entering. The Holy One heard his plea and sent Metatron, the Prince of the Presence, a great and exalted angel who serves closest to God's glory.

Metatron, shining with brilliant light, spread his wings in obedience and came down to meet Rabbi Ishmael. Taking his hand with strength yet gentleness, Metatron reassured him in the presence of the other heavenly beings, saying, "Come in peace before the great and mighty King, and behold the splendor of the

Merkaba." With that, Rabbi Ishmael was led into the seventh Hall and brought before the dwelling place of the Divine Presence, where he stood before the Holy One and witnessed the incredible vision of the Merkaba.

The heavenly rulers of the Merkaba and the fiery Seraphim looked upon him, their radiant glow and piercing gaze overwhelming him with fear and awe. Their presence was so powerful that he trembled and collapsed, unable to withstand their brilliance. His strength faded as he was overcome by the splendor of their faces and the overwhelming glory surrounding him.

Seeing this, the Holy One rebuked the Seraphim, Kerubim, and Ophannim, saying, "My servants, my Seraphim, my Kerubim, and my Ophannim, turn your eyes away from Ishmael, my son, my friend, my beloved one, and my glory, so that he will not tremble in fear before you."

At God's command, Metatron, the ever-faithful Prince of the Presence, stepped forward and restored Rabbi Ishmael's spirit. He helped him stand, but even then, Rabbi Ishmael was too weak to speak a single word of praise before the Throne of Glory. The moment was too powerful, and he remained silent in awe. Only after an hour had passed did he finally regain the strength to lift his voice in worship.

Then, the Holy One opened the heavenly gates before him. But these were not ordinary gates—they were the gates of Divine Presence, Peace, Wisdom, Strength, Power, Speech, Song, Holiness, and Praise. As these sacred gates opened, Rabbi Ishmael's eyes were filled with light, and his heart overflowed with praise. He lifted his voice and sang psalms, songs, and praises, pouring out words of thanksgiving, glory, and worship.

As Rabbi Ishmael lifted his voice in a song of devotion and awe before the Holy One, the heavenly Chayyoth, both above and below the Throne of Glory, joined in perfect harmony. Their voices echoed with powerful cries of "HOLY" and "BLESSED BE THE GLORY OF YHWH FROM HIS PLACE!" Together, their praises rose high, filling the heavens as a tribute to the endless majesty and glory of the Divine King.

Chapter II

Rabbi Ishmael described an incredible moment when the highest angels—the mighty eagles of the Merkaba, the fiery Ophannim, and the blazing Seraphim—began to question his presence. Their voices, filled with authority and devotion to God, called out to Metatron, the exalted Prince of the Presence. Their words carried both curiosity and amazement.

"Young one," they said, addressing Metatron with a title that reflected his strength and closeness to God. "Why do you allow a human, someone born on earth, to enter this holy place and witness the sacred vision of the Merkaba? Where is he from? What tribe does he belong to? What makes him worthy of such an honor?"

Metatron, always faithful to his role, answered with respect and confidence. "He is from the nation of Israel, the people chosen by the Holy One out of all seventy nations. This nation was set apart to carry His name and follow His commandments. He comes from the tribe of Levi, the tribe dedicated to God's service. He is a descendant of Aaron, whom the Holy One Himself chose and honored with the crown of priesthood at Mount Sinai."

When the angels heard this, they accepted his answer. Their awe turned into recognition, and they understood the privilege that had been given to Rabbi Ishmael. Their voices, now filled with praise, spoke of the holiness of Israel.

"Indeed," they said, "this man is worthy to see the Merkaba. Blessed is the nation that has him among their people."

Their words of joy and reverence echoed through the heavenly realms as they declared, "Happy is the people who are given such a blessing!" Their proclamation was not just about Rabbi Ishmael's honor—it was a reminder of the special connection between God and His people, a bond that sets apart those chosen to serve Him.

Chapter III

Metatron has seventy names, but God calls him "Youth."

Rabbi Ishmael said:

At that moment, I asked Metatron, the angel and Prince of the Presence, "What is your name?"

He answered, "I have seventy names, each one tied to the seventy languages of the world. But all of them are connected to my main name, Metatron, the angel of the Presence. However, my King calls me 'Youth' (Na'ar)."

Chapter IV

Metatron is the same as Enoch, who was taken to heaven before the Great Flood.

Rabbi Ishmael said:

I asked Metatron, "Why do you share a name with the Creator and have seventy different names? You are greater than all the heavenly rulers, higher than all the angels, and more beloved than any of God's servants. You have more power, authority, and glory than all the mighty ones. So why, in the highest heavens, are you still called 'Youth'?"

He answered, "I am Enoch, the son of Jared. When the people of the Flood turned away from God and lived in corruption, they rejected Him, saying, 'Leave us alone; we want nothing to do with Your ways' (Job 21:14). At that time, the Holy One took me from the world. He brought me to the heavens so that I could serve as a witness against them for all future generations. This way, no one could ever claim that God was unjust.

But why was everyone destroyed? What had their wives, children, or animals done? Why were their horses, mules, cattle, and all their possessions—even the birds—wiped out by the Flood? If the people had sinned, what wrong did the children commit? What could the animals and birds have done to deserve such destruction? How could anyone say it was fair that the innocent were punished along with the wicked?

Because of these questions, the Holy One took me up while the people were still alive, allowing them to witness my ascension. He made me a testimony to His justice. He then appointed me as a prince and leader among the ministering angels.

At that moment, three powerful angels—Uzza, Azza, and Azazel—stepped forward and accused me before the Holy One. They said, "Didn't the First Ones—the ancient angels—warn You not to create humans?"

The Holy One replied, "I created them, and I will take care of them. I will carry them, and I will save them" (Isaiah 46:4).

When the angels saw me, they protested, "Lord of the Universe! Why is this human allowed to rise to the heavens? Is he not a descendant of those who were destroyed in the Flood? Why has he been brought here?"

The Holy One responded, "Who are you to question Me? I find more joy in this one than in all of you. Therefore, he will be a prince and a ruler over you in the high heavens."

Immediately, the angels accepted God's decision. They came to me, bowed, and said, "Blessed are you, and blessed is your father, for your Creator has given you great honor."

And because I am still young compared to them in days, months, and years, they call me 'Youth' (Na'ar)."

Chapter V

The idolatry of Enosh's generation caused God to remove His presence from the earth.

Rabbi Ishmael said:

Metatron, the Prince of the Presence, explained to me:

From the day that the Holy One removed Adam from the Garden of Eden, His presence, the Shekina, remained on a Kerub beneath the Tree of Life. During that time, angels would descend from heaven in organized groups, traveling through the skies in great numbers to carry out His will across the world.

Adam and his descendants stood outside the gates of the Garden, gazing in awe at the brilliant light of the Shekina. Its radiance spread across the entire world, shining 3,000 times brighter than the sun. Anyone who stood in its light lived without suffering—there were no flies, no gnats, no sickness, no pain, and no harm from demons.

Whenever the Holy One moved—from the Garden to Eden, from Eden back to the Garden, then to the sky, and back again—His presence remained visible to all without causing harm. This divine light stayed on earth until the time of Enosh's generation, when people turned away from God and began worshiping idols.

What did the people of Enosh's time do? They traveled across the earth, gathering silver, gold, gems, and pearls. They built massive piles of treasure and used them to carve gigantic idols, each one as large as 1,000 parasangs. Around these idols, they placed the sun, moon, stars, and planets, believing these celestial forces would serve their idols just as they served the Holy One. Their actions reflected what is written in 1 Kings 22:19: "And all the host of heaven was standing by Him on His right hand and on His left."

But how did they accomplish such a thing? They could not have done this without the help of the fallen angels Azza, Uzza, and Azziel, who taught them the forbidden secrets of magic. Using these dark arts, they learned to control and manipulate heavenly forces to serve their idols.

At that time, the angels who served the Holy One brought their concerns before Him, saying, "Master of the World, why do You still care for humans? As it is written in Psalms 8:4, 'What is man (Enosh) that You are mindful of him?' It does not say 'What is Adam,' but 'What is Enosh,' for he has become the leader of idol worshippers.

Why have You left the highest heavens—the glorious realm where Your exalted Name is praised, the place of Your majestic and elevated Throne in Araboth? The heavens of Araboth, the highest of the heavens, are filled with Your splendor, might, and greatness. Your Throne there is lifted above all things.

And yet, You have come down to live among the children of men, who worship idols and compare You to their false gods. Now, You are on earth, but so are their lifeless idols. Why do You remain among people who have turned their backs on You?"

Immediately, the Holy One removed His Shekina from the earth and withdrew His presence from among them.

At that moment, the angels of heaven, along with the hosts and armies of Araboth—countless in number—gathered around the Shekina. They held trumpets and horns in their hands, forming a great procession as they lifted their voices in songs of praise. Surrounded by their music and worship, the Shekina rose to the highest heavens, just as it is written in Psalms 47:3:

"God has gone up with a shout, the Lord with the sound of a trumpet."

Chapter VI

Enoch Ascends to Heaven with the Shekina, and the Angels Question God

Rabbi Ishmael said:

Metatron, the Angel and Prince of the Presence, explained to me:

When the Holy One decided to bring me up to heaven, He first sent Metatron to carry out His command. In front of everyone around me, Metatron appeared and took me away. He carried me in a brilliant blaze of fire, riding on a chariot of flames pulled by fiery horses—servants of divine glory. Surrounded by a glowing light, I rose up and ascended together with the Shekina to the highest heavens.

As soon as I arrived, the holy angels—Chayyoth, Ophannim, Seraphim, Kerubim, and the Wheels of the Merkaba (the Galgallim)—along with the ministers of the fiery presence, became aware of me. They sensed my approach from an incredible distance—36,000 myriads of parasangs away. Smelling my essence, they were astonished and cried out in disbelief:

"What is this scent of a human? What is this trace of a mortal, formed from a tiny drop of flesh, daring to rise to the highest heavens? How can someone born of the earth enter this place and stand among those who are made of fire?"

Still amazed, they continued, saying:

"How can a being of flesh and blood reach this realm? How can a human, created from dust, stand among those who dwell in divine fire?"

Hearing their protests, the Holy One answered them:

"My servants, my heavenly hosts—my Kerubim, my Ophannim, my Seraphim—do not be troubled or upset by this! Listen carefully and understand. Nearly all the people on earth have turned away from Me. They have rejected My kingdom, abandoned My ways, and chosen to worship idols and false gods. Because of their actions, I have removed My Shekina from the earth and lifted it up to the heavens, far from them.

But this one is different. He is special, chosen, and precious among all who live on earth. He is unique, set apart by his faith, unwavering in righteousness, and pure in his actions. His devotion is greater than anyone else's, and he is worthy of this honor. I have taken him from the world as an offering—a soul of great value, chosen from all beneath the heavens to serve in My presence."

Chapter VII

Enoch Is Lifted to the Throne, the Merkaba, and the Angelic Hosts

Rabbi Ishmael said:

Metatron, the Angel and Prince of the Presence, explained to me:

When the Holy One decided to take me away from the generation of the Flood, He lifted me up on the wings of the Shekina's divine wind. Carried by this sacred force, I rose to the highest heavens, beyond anything that can be understood on earth. He brought me into the magnificent palaces of Araboth Raqia', a realm of incredible beauty and greatness.

There, I saw the glorious Throne of the Shekina, shining with a brilliance beyond words. Around it stood the great Merkaba, the divine chariot, surrounded by countless heavenly beings. I saw the troops of anger, fierce in their power, and the armies of judgment, ready to carry out God's will. Encircling the Throne were the fiery Shin'nim, beings of intense light, and the blazing Kerubim, whose radiance was beyond understanding.

The burning Ophannim, wheels of divine fire, moved with endless energy, while the flashing

Chashmallim sent out waves of glowing light and mystery. The Seraphim, creatures of pure lightning and flame, hovered nearby, their presence both overwhelming and humbling.

In the middle of this vast, heavenly assembly, the Holy One gave me a special and sacred role. He placed me before the Throne of Glory to serve and stand in His presence every day, witnessing the greatness and beauty that fill the highest heavens.

Chapter VIII

The gates of the treasuries of heaven opened to Metatron

Rabbi Ishmael said:

Metatron, the Prince of the Presence, told me:

Before the Holy One appointed me to serve at the Throne of Glory, He opened for me three hundred thousand gates of wisdom, understanding, kindness, love, humility, mercy, Torah, and reverence for heaven. Each gate unlocked a deeper level of knowledge and virtue, preparing me for my role.

At that moment, the Holy One increased my wisdom, adding layer upon layer of understanding. He deepened my awareness, sharpening my ability to see the finest details of divine truth. He filled me with knowledge upon knowledge, expanding my ability to comprehend His ways. He poured mercy upon mercy into me, strengthening my compassion for all creation. He gave me instruction upon instruction, enhancing my ability to teach and guide with absolute clarity.

He multiplied my love, making my heart overflow with kindness, and filled me with goodness upon goodness, creating an endless well of virtue within me.

He clothed me in humility upon humility, grounding my spirit in true meekness. He strengthened me with power upon power, increasing my abilities beyond understanding. He gave me might upon might, allowing me to stand firm and unwavering in my tasks. He filled me with light upon light, making my brilliance shine even brighter than before.

He enhanced my beauty, increasing it until I reflected the splendor of His presence. He covered me in glory upon glory, making me shine with the radiance of His greatness. With all these gifts, I was honored and blessed, receiving qualities greater than any of the children of heaven. He elevated me above them all, granting me virtues and wisdom beyond what any other heavenly being had ever received.

Chapter IX

Enoch Is Blessed and Transformed with Angelic Features

Rabbi Ishmael said: Metatron, the Prince of the Presence, explained to me:

After everything that had happened, the Holy One placed His hand upon me and gave me fifty-three unique blessings.

He then lifted me up and expanded my size until I stretched across the entire world, both in length and width.

He caused twenty-two wings to grow on me, with thirty-six wings on each side. Each wing was as vast as the whole world itself.

He gave me three hundred sixty-three eyes, and each one shined as brightly as the great light in the heavens.

He adorned me with unmatched splendor, brilliance, radiance, and beauty, filling me with the light of the entire universe. There was no form of majesty or glory that He did not place upon me.

Chapter X

God placed Metatron on a throne at the entrance of the highest hall and sent a messenger to announce his new role. Metatron was now God's representative, ruling over all the heavenly beings and the leaders of different realms—except for eight powerful princes who carried the sacred name of their King.

Rabbi Ishmael said: Metatron, the Prince of the Presence, explained to me:

"The Holy One, blessed be He, did all of this for me. He created a special throne for me, designed to look like the glorious Throne of God. He covered it with a curtain full of light, beauty, kindness, and mercy, shining just like the one before God's own throne. This curtain was decorated with all the lights of the universe, glowing in their full brilliance.

He placed this throne at the entrance of the Seventh Hall and seated me upon it. Then a messenger traveled through the heavens, declaring:

'This is Metatron, my servant. I have made him a prince and a ruler over all the leaders of my kingdoms and the heavenly beings—except for the eight great princes who bear the sacred name of their King.

From now on, any angel or prince who wishes to bring a matter before me must first go to him. They will speak to him, and he will represent them before me. Whatever command he gives in my name must be followed.

I have placed him under the care of the Prince of Wisdom and the Prince of Understanding, who will teach him the mysteries of heaven and earth, as well as the knowledge of this world and the next.

I have also put him in charge of all the treasuries in the heavenly palaces and all the stores of life that I possess in the highest heavens.'"

Chapter XI

God reveals all hidden knowledge to Metatron.

Rabbi Ishmael said: Metatron, the angel and Prince of the Presence, explained to me:

"From that moment on, the Holy One, blessed be He, showed me every mystery of the Torah and all the deepest secrets of wisdom. He let me understand the true depths of the Law, the thoughts of every living being, and the hidden truths of the universe. Every secret of Creation was made clear to me, just as they are fully known to the Creator Himself.

I carefully observed the mysteries of the universe and the wonders hidden within them. Before anyone even had a secret thought, I already knew it. Before something was created, I had already seen it.

There was nothing in the heavens above or in the depths below that was beyond my knowledge. Even before a person formed an idea, I understood their thoughts. Nothing in the highest places or the lowest depths was hidden from me."

Chapter XII

God gives Metatron a robe of glory, crowns him, and calls him "the Lesser VHWH."

Rabbi Ishmael said: Metatron, the Prince of the Presence, explained to me:

"Because of the deep love the Holy One, blessed be He, had for me—more than for any of the other heavenly beings—He made me a special garment of glory. This robe was covered in dazzling light, and He dressed me in it.

He also created a second robe for me, one of honor, decorated with beauty, brilliance, and majesty. Then, He placed it on me as well.

After that, He made a royal crown just for me. It was set with forty-nine precious stones, each glowing as brightly as the sun.

The light from this crown shone in every direction, spreading across the highest heavens, through all seven levels, and to the farthest corners of the world. Then, He placed it upon my head. Finally, in front of all the heavenly beings, He called me 'The Lesser VHWH,' as it is written in Exodus 23:21: 'For My Name is in him.'"

Chapter XIII

God writes the letters of creation on Metatron's crown with a flaming pen.

Rabbi Ishmael said: Metatron, the angel and Prince of the Presence, explained to me:

"Because of the great love and kindness the Holy One, blessed be He, had for me—more than for any other heavenly being—He used His own finger to write on the crown placed upon my head. With a pen of fire, He engraved the sacred letters by which the heavens and the earth were created.

These same letters brought the seas, rivers, mountains, and hills into existence. They shaped the planets, stars, and all the forces of nature. The winds, lightning, earthquakes, and thunder came from them, as did snow, hail, and storms. Every element of the world and the entire structure of Creation was formed by these letters.

Each letter on my crown glowed with an unending light. At times, they flashed like lightning. Other times, they burned like torches or flickered like flames. Their brightness was as powerful as the sun, the moon, and the stars, shining across the heavens.

When the Holy One, blessed be He, placed this crown upon my head, all the rulers of the heavenly realms trembled before me. The highest princes and the strongest angels—those greater than all the others who stand before God's Throne—shook with fear.

Even Sammael, the Prince of the Accusers, the mightiest of all the rulers of the heavens, was filled with dread when he saw me.

The angels who govern the forces of nature—the angel of fire, the angel of hail, the angel of wind, the angel of lightning, the angel of wrath, the angel of thunder, the angel of snow, the angel of rain, the angel of the day, the angel of the night, the angel of the sun, the angel of the moon, the angel of the planets, and the angel of the stars—all of them, powerful in their own right, trembled at the sight of me.

These rulers of the world have names:

- Gabriel, ruler of fire
- Baradiel, ruler of hail
- Ruchiel, ruler of the wind
- Baragiel, ruler of lightning
- Za'amiel, ruler of wrath
- Ziqiel, ruler of sparks
- Zi'iel, ruler of disturbances
- Za'aphiel, ruler of storms

- Ra'amiel, ruler of thunder
- Ra'ashiel, ruler of earthquakes
- Shafgiel, ruler of snow
- Matariel, ruler of rain
- Shimshiel, ruler of the day
- Lailiel, ruler of the night
- Galgalliel, ruler of the sun
- 'Ophanniel, ruler of the moon
- Kohbiel, ruler of the planets
- Rahatiel, ruler of the stars

When all these powerful beings saw me, they fell to the ground, unable to look at me. The dazzling light that shone from the crown on my head was so overwhelming that they were struck with awe, unable to lift their eyes to meet mine."

Chapter XIV

Metatron Transformed into Fire

Rabbi Ishmael said: Metatron, the angel and Prince of the Presence, explained to me:

"When the Holy One, blessed be He, chose me to serve at His Throne of Glory, to assist with the divine chariot and the presence of His majesty, my very being was transformed. My body turned into flames of fire, my muscles became blazing sparks, and my bones glowed like burning coals. The light from my eyelids flashed like lightning, my eyes burned like fiery embers, and my hair became flames. Every part of me turned into wings of fire, and my whole form radiated with intense heat.

On my right, streams of fire flowed endlessly, and on my left, burning flames erupted. Stormwinds and tempests surrounded me, while the sound of roaring thunder and shaking earth echoed before and behind me."

Rabbi Ishmael said: Metatron, the highest of all princes, stands before the One greater than all other powers. He moves beneath the Throne of Glory and dwells in a magnificent home of light above. From there, he gathers the fire of deafness and places it into the ears of the heavenly creatures, so they cannot hear the overwhelming voice of God's word.

When Moses climbed to the heights, he fasted for forty days and nights until the secret places of divine energy were revealed to him. He saw the purest, deepest heart within the heart of the Lion, shining as white as its very core. Around him stood countless angels, their presence filled with blazing fire, and they longed to consume him. But Moses prayed—first for the people of Israel and then for himself.

The One who sits upon the divine chariot opened the windows above the cherubim. A vast group of 1,800 angelic beings, along with Metatron, the Prince of the Presence, came out to meet Moses. They gathered the prayers of Israel, shaped them into a crown, and placed it upon the head of the Holy One, blessed be He.

Then they proclaimed, "Hear, O Israel: the Lord our God, the Lord is One." Their faces shone with joy, and the Divine Presence radiated with brilliant light. The Shekina rejoiced, and the angels asked Metatron, "What is this great honor? Who is it for?" The answer came: "It is for the Glorious Lord of Israel."

They declared again, "Hear, O Israel: the Lord our God is One, the Eternal King who lives forever."

At that moment, Akatriel Yah Yehod Sebaoth spoke to Metatron and commanded, "Let no prayer from Moses go unanswered. Listen to his requests and grant them, no matter how big or small."

Then Metatron turned to Moses and said, "Son of Amram, do not be afraid. God is pleased with you! Ask for whatever you desire from His Glory. Your face shines with a light that stretches across the world."

But Moses hesitated. "I fear that I might bring guilt upon myself," he said.

Metatron reassured him, "Take hold of the sacred letters of the oath. They are unbreakable and guarantee that the covenant will never be broken."

Chapter XV

Metatron Divested of His Privilege of Presiding on a Throne of His Own on Account of Acher's Misunderstanding, Thinking Him a Second Divine Power

Rabbi Ishmael said: Metatron, the angel and Prince of the Presence, explained to me:

"At first, I sat on a great throne at the entrance of the Seventh Hall. From there, I carried out judgments for the heavenly beings, ruling over the divine hosts under the authority of the Holy One, blessed be He. I was given the power to grant greatness, kingship, honor, rulership, and glory to the princes of the heavenly realms. While overseeing the Celestial Court, I remained seated, while the princes of the kingdoms stood before me—some to my right and others to my left—all by the command of the Holy One.

But when Acher entered and saw the vision of the divine chariot, he became overwhelmed with fear. His soul trembled, and he nearly lost himself, overcome by terror and awe. He saw me seated on a throne like a king, with countless angels standing around me as attendants. The crowned rulers of the heavens stood in my presence, and the sight filled him with confusion and dread.

In his shock, he spoke aloud and said, 'Surely, there must be two divine powers in heaven!'

Immediately, a divine voice rang out from heaven, from the presence of the Shekina, declaring: 'Return, O wayward children—except for Acher!'

Then Aniyel, a mighty and honored prince, a being of great majesty and power, was sent on a mission from the Holy One, blessed be He. He struck me sixty times with lashes of fire and commanded me to rise to my feet."

Chapter XVI

The Princes of the Seven Heavens, of the Sun, Moon, Planets, and Constellations and Their Hosts of Angels

Rabbi Ishmael said: Metatron, the angel and Prince of the Presence, explained to me:

"There are seven great princes, each of them magnificent, respected, and full of wonder. They have been placed in charge of the seven heavens. Their names are Mikael, Gabriel, Shatqiel, Shachaqiel, Bakariel, Badariel, and Pachriel.

Each of these princes rules over a different heaven and leads a vast host of 496,000 groups of ministering angels.

- Mikael, the highest prince, governs the seventh and highest heaven, Araboth.
- Gabriel, leader of the heavenly armies, rules over the sixth heaven, Maban.
- Shatqiel, another powerful prince, is in charge of the fifth heaven, Ma'an.
- Shachaqiel oversees the fourth heaven, Ja'uf.
- Badariel commands the third heaven, Shejaqim.
- Barakiel rules over the second heaven, Raqia'.

- Pachriel governs the first heaven, Wilan, which is within Shamayim.

Below them is Algalliel, the prince responsible for the movement of the sun. He is accompanied by 96 great and honored angels who guide the sun's path through the heavens of Raqia'.

Beneath them is Ophanniel, the prince who controls the moon's journey. With him are 84 angels who move the moon along its orbit. Each night, they guide it 354,000 parasangs, especially on the fifteenth day of the month when it reaches its turning point in the East.

Next is Rahatiel, the prince in charge of the stars and constellations. He is assisted by seven great and powerful angels. His name, Rahatiel, comes from his task—guiding the stars as they move through the sky. Each night, he leads them 339,000 parasangs, moving them from East to West and back again. The Holy One, blessed be He, has created a special path for them—a place where the sun, moon, planets, and stars rest as they travel from West to East during the night.

Following him is Kokbiel, the prince who rules over the planets. With him are 354,000 groups of ministering angels. These powerful angels guide the planets, moving them from one city and province to another within the heavens of Raqia'.

Above them all are seventy-two princes of the heavenly kingdoms, each corresponding to one of the seventy languages spoken on Earth. These princes wear royal crowns, are dressed in robes of honor, and are wrapped in magnificent cloaks. They ride royal horses and carry scepters, displaying their great authority.

As they travel through the heavens, servants run ahead of them, announcing their arrival with grand celebration. Just as earthly rulers travel with chariots, horsemen, and great armies, so do these heavenly princes make their way through Raqia'. Their journeys are marked with majesty, splendor, songs of praise, and honor. Vast armies of angels accompany them, singing and rejoicing in their greatness, just as people do when earthly kings travel in magnificent processions."

Chapter XVII

The order of ranks of the angels and the homage received by the higher ranks from the lower ones

Rabbi Ishmael said: Metatron, the angel and Prince of the Presence, explained to me:

"The angels of the first heaven, whenever they see their prince, immediately get off their heavenly horses and bow down, pressing their faces to the ground in respect. The prince of the first heaven, when he sees the prince of the second heaven, also dismounts, removes his crown, and falls on his face in humility.

The prince of the second heaven, upon seeing the prince of the third heaven, takes off his crown and bows down in awe. Likewise, the prince of the third heaven, when he sees the prince of the fourth heaven, removes his crown and lowers himself to the ground in deep respect.

The prince of the fourth heaven, when he meets the prince of the fifth heaven, does the same—removing his crown and bowing with his face to the ground. The prince of the fifth heaven, upon seeing the prince of the sixth heaven, also removes his crown and falls on his face in reverence.

The prince of the sixth heaven, when he sees the prince of the seventh heaven, takes off his crown and bows, trembling with awe. The prince of the seventh heaven, upon meeting the seventy-two princes of the heavenly kingdoms, removes his crown and falls on his face in deep humility.

The seventy-two princes, when they approach the gatekeepers of the first hall in the highest heaven, Araboth Raqia', remove their crowns and bow low in honor.

The gatekeepers of the first hall, when they see the gatekeepers of the second hall, also take off their crowns and lower themselves to the ground. The gatekeepers of the second hall, upon meeting those of the third hall, do the same—removing their crowns and bowing in respect.

This continues at every level:

- The gatekeepers of the third hall bow before those of the fourth hall.
- The fourth hall's gatekeepers bow before those of the fifth.
- The fifth hall's gatekeepers lower themselves before the sixth.
- The sixth hall's gatekeepers fall on their faces before those of the seventh.

When the gatekeepers of the seventh hall see the four great princes—the most honored ones, appointed over the four camps of the Divine Presence—they take off their crowns and bow in complete submission.

The four great princes, when they see the highest prince—the one who leads all of heaven in song and praise—remove their crowns and lower their faces to the ground in worship.

Tag'as, the great and honored prince, when he encounters Barattiel, the mighty prince who stands three fingers high in the highest heaven, Araboth, removes his crown and bows deeply to the ground.

Barattiel, when he sees Hamon, the powerful and revered prince, who is both awe-inspiring and magnificent—so powerful that all of heaven trembles when he calls out the 'Thrice Holy'—removes his crown and falls on his face in fear and respect.

Hamon, when he meets Tutresiel, another mighty prince, takes off his crown and bows to the ground. Tutresiel, when he sees Atrugiel, the great prince, also removes his crown and lowers his face in deep reverence."

Atrugiel, the great prince, when he sees Na'aririel, another great prince, removes his crown and bows down with his face to the ground.

Na'aririel, when he meets Sasnigiel, takes off his crown and lowers himself in respect. Sasnigiel, upon seeing Zazriel, removes his crown and bows deeply to show honor. Zazriel, when he encounters Geburatiel, does the same—taking off his crown and falling on his face in humility.

Geburatiel, when he sees 'Anaphiel, removes his crown and bows low. 'Anaphiel, when he meets Ashruylu, the prince who oversees all heavenly gatherings, also removes his crown and lowers himself in submission.

Ashruylu, when he sees Callisur, the prince who reveals the secrets of the divine law, takes off his crown and bows with his face to the ground in reverence. Callisur, when he meets Zakzakiel, the prince responsible for recording Israel's deeds before the Throne of Glory, removes his crown and falls on his face in humility.

Zakzakiel, upon seeing 'Anaphiel, the prince who holds the keys to the heavenly halls, also removes his crown and bows low. Why is he called 'Anaphiel? Because his honor, brilliance, and majestic presence spread throughout all the heavenly chambers, much like the Creator's glory fills the universe, as written in Habakkuk 3:3: "His glory covered the heavens, and the earth was full of His praise." In the same way,

'Anaphiel's greatness overshadows all the splendor of Araboth, the highest heaven.

When 'Anaphiel sees Sother Ashiel, a mighty and revered prince, he removes his crown and lowers himself in awe. Why is he called Sother Ashiel? Because he is in charge of the four streams of the fiery river that flows before the Throne of Glory. Every heavenly being must have his permission to enter or leave the presence of the Divine. He controls the seals of the fiery river, and his towering height measures 7,000 myriads of parasangs. When he moves before the Divine Presence, he stirs the flames of the river and declares what is written about the deeds of the world, as described in Daniel 7:10: "The judgment was set, and the books were opened."

Sother Ashiel, when he sees Shoqed Chozi, a powerful and fearsome prince, removes his crown and bows low. Why is Shoqed Chozi given this name? Because he weighs all human actions on a balance before the Holy One, blessed be He.

When Shoqed Chozi sees Zehanpuryu, a mighty and honored prince feared by all the heavenly hosts, he takes off his crown and bows in humility. Why is Zehanpuryu called by this name? Because he has the power to command the fiery river and send it back to its source.

When Zehanpuryu sees Azbuga, a prince greatly revered and exalted among those who understand the mysteries of the Throne of Glory, he removes his crown and bows down in awe. Why is Azbuga called by this name? Because in the future, he will clothe the righteous in garments of life and wrap them in robes of light, preparing them for eternal life.

When Azbuga sees two great and powerful princes standing above him, he removes his crown and falls to the ground in deep respect. These two princes are known as Sopheriel H' the Killer and Sopheriel H' the Lifegiver. Both are ancient, mighty, and beyond reproach.

Why is one called Sopheriel H' the Killer? Because he is responsible for the book of the dead, recording the names of those whose time has come. Why is the other called Sopheriel H' the Lifegiver? Because he oversees the book of life, where the names of those whom God grants life are written, according to His will.

You may wonder, "Since God sits on a throne, do these princes also sit while writing?" The Scriptures teach (1 Kings 22:19, 2 Chronicles 18:18): "And all the host of heaven stands by Him." This makes it clear that even the greatest heavenly beings perform their duties while standing.

But how do they write while standing? One stands on the wheels of a storm, and the other stands on the wheels of a whirlwind. They wear royal garments and are wrapped in majestic cloaks. Both wear crowns of glory. Their entire bodies are covered in eyes, and they shine as brightly as lightning. Their eyes glow like the sun at full strength, and their height stretches across all seven heavens. Their wings are as numerous as the days of the year and spread across the entire expanse of the sky.

Their lips are as wide as the gates of the East, and their tongues rise as high as the waves of the ocean. Flames pour from their mouths, and their tongues burn like torches. A sapphire stone rests on each of their heads, and on their shoulders are wheels driven by swift cherubim. One holds a fiery scroll, while the other holds a flaming pen. The scroll is 30,000 myriads of parasangs long, the pen measures 3,000 myriads, and each letter they write is 365 parasangs in size.

Chapter XVIII

Ribbiel, the Prince of the Wheels of the Merkaba, and the Surroundings of the Merkaba. The Commotion Among the Angelic Hosts During the Qedushsha

Rabbi Ishmael said: Metatron, the angel and Prince of the Presence, explained to me:

"Above these three powerful angels, there is one prince who stands apart from all others. He is honored, noble, and glorious, feared for his strength and might. He is magnificent, crowned with greatness, exalted, and beloved. There is no other prince like him. His name is Ribbiel, the great and revered prince who stands by the divine chariot.

Why is he called Ribbiel? Because he has been given authority over the wheels of the divine chariot, and they are under his control.

How many wheels are there? There are eight in total—two in each direction. Around them are four powerful winds, each with its own name: Storm Wind, Tempest, Strong Wind, and Wind of Earthquake.

Beneath the wheels, four fiery rivers flow, one on each side. Between these rivers stand four massive clouds. These clouds are known as clouds of fire, clouds of lamps, clouds of coal, and clouds of brimstone. Positioned around the wheels, they create a scene of overwhelming power and energy.

The feet of the heavenly creatures rest upon these wheels. Between each wheel, the sound of roaring earthquakes and crashing thunder echoes through the heavens.

When the moment comes for the great Song to be sung, the wheels begin to move, and the clouds shake.

At that time, all of heaven trembles:

- The mighty leaders become afraid.
- The horsemen grow restless.
- The warriors are shaken.
- The heavenly armies are filled with fear.
- The ranks of angels are overwhelmed.
- The appointed ones rush away in alarm.
- The commanders and soldiers are filled with dread.
- The servants grow weak.
- Every angel and heavenly division trembles in awe.

As the wheels turn, they call out to one another. One crown speaks to another, one heavenly creature calls to the next, and one Seraph reaches out to another, saying, as it is written in Psalm 68:3:

'Praise Him who rides upon the heavens, by His name Yah, and rejoice before Him!'"

Chapter XIX

Rabbi Ishmael said: Metatron, the angel and Prince of the Presence, explained to me:

"Above all these stands one great and powerful prince. His name is Chayy'liel. He is noble and honored, full of strength and glory. He is so mighty that all the heavenly beings tremble before him. His power is so great that he could swallow the entire earth in a single moment, as if with one bite.

Why is he called Chayy'liel? Because he has been placed in charge of the Holy Chayyoth. He strikes them with lashes of fire to stir them into action, and when they sing praises, he honors them. He urges them to proclaim, 'Holy, holy, holy,' and 'Blessed be the glory of the Lord from His place!' during the great hymn of praise."

Chapter XX

The Chayyoth

Rabbi Ishmael said: Metatron, the angel and Prince of the Presence, explained to me:

"There are four great heavenly beings, called the Chayyoth, each connected to one of the four winds. Every one of them is as vast as the entire world. Each has four faces, and all their faces look toward the East.

Each Chayyâ has four enormous wings, each as large as the roof of the universe. Their faces contain even more faces within them, and their wings have layers upon layers of wings. The size of their faces is equal to 248 faces, and their wings are as massive as 363 wings combined.

Each of these beings wears 2,000 crowns on its head. Every crown is as beautiful as a rainbow in the sky and shines as brightly as the sun. Sparks of light radiate from them, glowing like the morning star, the planet Venus, as it rises in the East."

Chapter XXI (A)

Kerubiel, the Prince of the Kerubim, and the Description of the Kerubim

Rabbi Ishmael said: Metatron, the angel and Prince of the Presence, explained to me:

"Above all these stands one great and powerful prince. His name is Kerubiel, a noble and honored leader, full of strength and glory. His power and majesty surpass all others. He is lifted high, a righteous and holy prince, praised in every way.

Thousands of hosts celebrate him, and tens of thousands of armies exalt him. When he is angry, the earth trembles. When he is filled with wrath, the heavens shake. His presence alone causes the foundations of creation to quake, and at his rebuke, even the highest heavens tremble.

His entire body glows with burning coals. His height stretches across the seven heavens, his width spans them completely, and his form is as vast as the entirety of the heavens themselves.

When he opens his mouth, it shines like a fiery lamp, and his tongue blazes like a consuming fire. His eyebrows flash like lightning, his eyes glow with dazzling sparks, and his face burns like a raging fire.

On his head, he wears a crown of holiness, engraved with the sacred Name, from which lightning flashes forth. A divine bow rests between his shoulders. At his waist is a mighty sword, and arrows of blazing fire are strapped to his side. A shield of consuming flames hangs around his neck, surrounded by glowing coals, which encircle him completely.

The brilliance of the Divine Presence shines from his face. Majestic horns rise from his wheels, and a royal diadem rests upon his head.

His entire body is covered in countless eyes, and great wings stretch across his towering form. A burning flame rises on his right, while a fire glows on his left, with coals constantly smoldering. Firebrands erupt from his body, lightning flashes from his face, thunder echoes around him, and earthquakes rumble at his side.

Two powerful princes of the divine chariot remain beside him at all times.

Why is he called Kerubiel? Because he is in charge of the chariot of the Kerubim, the mighty beings under his command. He decorates their crowns and polishes the diadems on their heads.

He enhances their beauty and strengthens their glory. He increases their honor and leads their praise. He magnifies their splendor and refines their radiant majesty. He arranges their songs of worship to prepare a dwelling place for the One who sits upon the Kerubim.

The Kerubim stand beside the Holy Chayyoth, their wings raised high, reaching the tops of their heads. The Divine Presence rests upon them, and the brilliance of Glory shines on their faces. Songs of praise flow from their mouths, their hands are hidden beneath their wings, and their feet are covered as well. Majestic horns rise from their heads, and the light of the Divine Presence radiates from their faces.

Around them are sapphire stones and columns of fire, burning on all four sides. Fiery pillars stand beside them. A sapphire rests on one side and another on the opposite side, with glowing coals beneath them.

In every direction, divine signs stand, while their wings interlock above their heads in a display of majesty. They spread their wings in praise of the One who rides upon the clouds and glorify the awe-inspiring King of Kings.

Kerubiel, the prince who rules over them, arranges them in perfect harmony. He lifts them to new heights of honor and splendor. He strengthens them with power and beauty so they can fulfill the will of their

Creator at all times. Above their exalted heads, the glory of the High King, who dwells upon the Kerubim, shines without end."

Chapter XXI (B)

Rabbi Ishmael said: Metatron, the angel, the Prince of the Presence, explained to me:

There is a great court before the Throne of Glory.

How do the angels stand in the heights of heaven? He said: They stand like a vast and endless bridge, stretching as if over a great river. No seraph or angel is assigned to rule over it; all may approach, but the distance to cross it is enormous, measuring 30,000 parasangs. Other bridges, just as massive, extend across countless parasangs, from one end to the other. As it is written in Isaiah 6:2: "And the Seraphim stand above it and proclaim a song before Him."

The last word of this verse has a numerical value of 86, which matches the sacred name YHWH, the God of Israel. Standing before His Throne are powerful and fearsome beings—thousands upon thousands, and ten thousand times ten thousand. They lift their voices in songs of praise and worship before YHWH, the God of Israel.

The sacred text also reveals the number of bridges that exist in the heavens. There are many different kinds: bridges of fire, bridges of hail, and also rivers of hail.

There are treasuries of snow and spinning wheels of fire.

There are 24 myriads of these fiery wheels. The ministering angels number 12,000 myriads—6,000 myriads above and 6,000 myriads below. In the same way, there are 12,000 rivers of hail and 12,000 treasuries of snow, equally divided—6,000 above and 6,000 below. The 24 myriads of fiery wheels are also split evenly, 12 above and 12 below. They surround the bridges, the rivers of fire, and the rivers of hail. Many ministering angels create paths through them, guiding all who stand in their midst, aligning their power with the roads of the heavens.

What does YHWH, the God of Israel, the King of Glory, do? The Great and Fearsome One, mighty in strength, hides His face.

In the highest heaven, Araboth, there are 660,000 myriads of glorious angels standing before the Throne of Glory, surrounded by blazing divisions of fire. The King of Glory covers His face, for if He did not, the heavens themselves would be torn apart by the overwhelming brilliance, majesty, beauty, and holiness of the Holy One, blessed be He.

Countless ministering angels carry out His will. There are unnumbered kings and rulers in Araboth, dwelling in His divine presence. These are honored angels among the leaders of the heavens, singing praises and remembering love. They tremble in awe of the splendor of the Divine Presence, their eyes blinded by the shining beauty of their King. Their faces darken, and their strength fades before Him.

From His Throne, rivers of joy pour forth—streams of gladness, rivers of celebration, streams of triumph, rivers of love, and currents of friendship. These waters grow stronger as they flow, surging through the gates of Araboth, carrying a mighty sound. They are accompanied by the voices of the Chayyoth marching and calling out, by the joyful tambourines of the Ophannim, and by the ringing cymbals of the Kerubim.

As these rivers swell, they rise with the song:

"HOLY, HOLY, HOLY IS THE LORD OF HOSTS; THE WHOLE EARTH IS FILLED WITH HIS GLORY."

Chapter XXI (C)

Rabbi Ishmael said: Metatron, the Prince of the Presence, explained to me:

The distance between each bridge is 12 myriads of parasangs. The path leading up spans 12 myriads of parasangs, and the path going down is the same.

The space between the rivers of dread and the rivers of fear is 22 myriads of parasangs. The distance between the rivers of hail and the rivers of darkness is 33 myriads. From the chambers of lightning to the clouds of compassion, it is 42 myriads. The clouds of compassion are 84 myriads away from the divine chariot. From the divine chariot to the Kerubim, the distance is 148 myriads. Between the Kerubim and the Ophannim, there are 24 myriads, and from the Ophannim to the inner chambers, the distance is also 24 myriads. From the inner chambers to the Holy Chayyoth, the span is 100,000 myriads of parasangs.

The space between the wings of the Chayyoth measures 12 myriads, and the width of each wing is the same. The distance between the Holy Chayyoth and the Throne of Glory stretches 130,000 myriads of parasangs.

From the base of the Throne to its seat, there are 40,000 myriads of parasangs. And the name of the One who sits upon it—let His name be made holy!

The arches of the Bow rise high above the heavens, reaching 1,000 thousands and 10,000 times ten thousands of parasangs in height. Their size matches the measure of the Irin and Qaddishin, the Warriors and Holy Ones. As it is written in Genesis 9:13: "My bow I have set in the cloud." It does not say "I will set," but "I have set," meaning it is already placed. These clouds surround the Throne of Glory, and as they pass by, the angels of hail are transformed into burning coals.

The fire of the divine voice descends from the Holy Chayyoth, but because of its power, the Chayyoth run to another place, fearing they might be sent forth. Yet they return quickly, afraid of judgment from the other side. This is why it is said in Ezekiel 1:14, "They run and return."

The arches of the Bow shine more brilliantly than the summer sun at its peak. They glow brighter than blazing fire, and their beauty and radiance have no equal. Above the arches of the Bow stand the wheels of the Ophannim. Their height measures 1,000 thousands and 10,000 times ten thousands of parasangs, matching the measure of the Seraphim and the Heavenly Troops."

Chapter XXII

The winds blowing under the wings of the Kerubim

Rabbi Ishmael said: Metatron, the angel and Prince of the Presence, explained to me:

"Beneath the wings of the Kerubim, many different winds blow. Among them is the Brooding Wind, as it is written in Genesis 1:2: 'And the wind of God was brooding over the waters.'

There is also the Strong Wind, mentioned in Exodus 14:21: 'And the Lord caused the sea to go back by a strong east wind all that night.'

The East Wind is another, as written in Exodus 10:13: 'The east wind brought the locusts.'

The Wind of Quails is described in Numbers 11:31: 'And there went forth a wind from the Lord and brought quails.'

The Wind of Jealousy is also among them, as mentioned in Numbers 5:14: 'And the wind of jealousy came upon him.'

The Wind of Earthquake appears in 1 Kings 19:11: 'After that came the wind of the earthquake, but the Lord was not in the earthquake.'

The Wind of the Lord is described in Ezekiel 37:1: 'And He carried me out by the wind of the Lord and set me down.'

There is also the Evil Wind, as written in 1 Samuel 16:23: 'And the evil wind departed from him.'

Other winds include the Wind of Wisdom, Wind of Understanding, Wind of Knowledge, and Wind of the Fear of the Lord, as Isaiah 11:2 states: 'And the wind of the Lord shall rest upon him—the wind of wisdom and understanding, the wind of counsel and might, the wind of knowledge and the fear of the Lord.'

The Wind of Rain is found in Proverbs 25:23: 'The north wind brings forth rain.'

The Wind of Lightnings is mentioned in Jeremiah 10:13 and 51:16: 'He makes lightnings for the rain and brings forth the wind out of His treasuries.'

The Wind that Breaks the Rocks is described in 1 Kings 19:11: 'The Lord passed by, and a great and strong wind tore through the mountains and shattered the rocks before the Lord.'

The Wind that Calms the Sea is found in Genesis 8:1: 'And God made a wind pass over the earth, and the waters subsided.'

The Wind of Wrath appears in Job 1:19: 'And behold, there came a great wind from the wilderness, striking the four corners of the house, and it collapsed.'

The Storm-Wind is mentioned in Psalm 148:8: 'Storm-wind, fulfilling His word.'

Satan is also connected to these winds, as Storm-Wind is sometimes linked to him. But all of these winds move only beneath the wings of the Kerubim, as Psalm 18:11 says: 'And He rode upon a cherub and flew; yes, He soared upon the wings of the wind.'

Where do these winds go? Scripture explains that they emerge from beneath the wings of the Kerubim and travel to the globe of the sun, as Ecclesiastes 1:6 states: 'The wind moves toward the south and turns toward the north; it continues its cycle, returning to where it started.'

From the sun, they flow to the rivers and seas, then move across the mountains and hills, as written in Amos 4:13: 'For behold, He who forms the mountains and creates the wind.'

From the mountains and hills, they return to the seas and rivers. From the seas and rivers, they pass over cities and lands. From the cities, they enter the Garden, and from the Garden, they reach Eden, as Genesis 3:8 says: 'Walking in the Garden in the wind of the day.'

Inside the Garden, the winds blend together, moving back and forth. They absorb the fragrance of the spices from every corner of the Garden. Then, they spread out again, carrying this pure scent. This fragrance is brought from the farthest parts of Eden to the righteous, who will one day inherit the Garden of Eden and the Tree of Life, as written in Song of Songs 4:16:

'Awake, O north wind; and come, O south wind! Blow upon my garden, that its spices may flow out. Let my beloved enter his garden and eat its precious fruits.'"

Chapter XXIII

The different chariots of the Holy One, blessed be He

Rabbi Ishmael said: Metatron, the angel and Prince of the Presence, explained to me:

"The Holy One, blessed be He, has many different kinds of chariots.

He has the Chariots of the Kerubim, as written in Psalm 18:11 and 2 Samuel 22:11: 'And He rode upon a cherub and flew.' These chariots are carried by the powerful and glorious Kerubim, who bear the divine presence and swiftly transport Him through the heavens.

He has the Chariots of Wind, as written in Psalm 18:10: 'And He flew swiftly upon the wings of the wind.' These chariots move as fast as the wind, carried by the forces of nature across all creation.

He has the Chariots of the Swift Cloud, as written in Isaiah 19:1: 'Behold, the Lord rides upon a swift cloud.' These chariots travel through the skies on clouds, representing divine majesty and swift judgment.

He has the Chariots of Clouds, as written in Exodus 19:9: 'Lo, I come unto you in a cloud.' Surrounded by clouds of glory, these chariots reveal His presence in mystery and splendor.

He has the Chariots of the Altar, as written in Amos 9:1: 'I saw the Lord standing upon the altar.' These chariots connect heaven and sacred places on earth, where He meets with His people.

He has the Chariots of Ribbotaim, as written in Psalm 68:18: 'The chariots of God are Ribbotaim, thousands upon thousands.' These chariots are surrounded by endless multitudes of angels, showing His unlimited power.

He has the Chariots of the Tent, as written in Deuteronomy 31:1: 'And the Lord appeared in the Tent in a pillar of cloud.' These chariots signify His presence in the Tent of Meeting, where He spoke with His people.

Each of these chariots serves a special purpose, displaying His majesty, strength, and presence as He moves through the heavens and interacts with creation.

He has the Chariots of the Tabernacle, as written in Leviticus: 'And the Lord spoke to him out of the tabernacle.' These chariots reveal His presence within the sacred space of the tabernacle, where He communicates His will.

He has the Chariots of the Mercy Seat, as written in Numbers: 'Then he heard the voice speaking to him from above the mercy seat.' These chariots represent the place where divine mercy and guidance are given.

He has the Chariots of Sapphire Stone, as written in Exodus: 'And under His feet was something like a pavement of sapphire stone.' These chariots shine with the brilliance of sapphire, symbolizing purity and heavenly majesty.

He has the Chariots of Eagles, as written in Exodus: 'I bore you on eagles' wings.' This does not mean actual eagles but refers to the speed and strength of those who carry His presence swiftly and powerfully.

He has the Chariots of Shout, as written in Psalms: 'God has gone up with a shout.' These chariots carry the triumphant and joyful proclamation of His glory through the heavens.

He has the Chariots of Araboth, as written in Psalms: 'Extol Him who rides upon the Araboth.' These chariots exist in the highest heavens, carrying His presence through the exalted realms.

He has the Chariots of Thick Clouds, as written in Psalms: 'He makes the thick clouds His chariot.' These chariots are hidden by clouds, showing the mystery and awe of His presence.

He has the Chariots of the Chayyoth, as written in Ezekiel: 'And the Chayyoth ran and returned.' These chariots, powered by the Holy Chayyoth, only move by divine command, as the Shekinah rests above them.

He has the Chariots of Wheels, as written in Ezekiel: 'And he said: Go in between the whirling wheels.' These chariots, moved by celestial wheels, represent divine power and movement.

He has the Chariots of a Swift Cherub, as written: 'Riding on a swift cherub.' When He rides upon a cherub, He places one foot upon it, and before setting the other foot down, He looks across eighteen thousand worlds. In that single moment, He sees and understands everything within them, as written in Psalms: 'You know my sitting down and my rising up; You understand my thoughts from afar.' Nothing in creation is hidden from Him.

Think of how much He perceives in just that instant, between one step and the next. When He rides upon the cherub and descends, His glory fills all creation. Then He rises again to His place. Everything exists because of His word, as written in Psalms: 'By the word of the Lord, the heavens were made.'

Who can count the number of His chariots? Scripture teaches that all these chariots stand before Him, ready to serve. There are countless myriads upon myriads of them.

The One who rides upon them knows their exact

number. He has the power to set His foot upon them, and they bow before Him in complete submission, as written in Psalms: 'If I ascend into heaven, You are there; if I make my bed in the depths, You are there.'

When He rides upon the Kerubim, they carry Him. He moves upon their wings and dwells among them, yet they remain His servants, fulfilling His will.

All these chariots are bound by a divine oath to serve Him. With a single glance, He sees all of creation and rules over it. The chariots move at His command, without hesitation.

When He calls them, they respond instantly. They hear His voice, rush to carry out His will, and glorify the name of the Holy One, blessed be He."

Chapter XXIV

'Ophanniel, the Triune of the 'Ophannim

Rabbi Ishmael said: Metatron, the angel and Prince of the Presence, explained to me:

"Above all these beings, there is a powerful and exalted prince, ancient and mighty. His name is 'Ophanniel.

He has sixteen faces—four on each side—and one hundred wings on each side of his body. His form is covered with 8,466 eyes, matching the number of days in the year.

Each of his two front-facing eyes flashes with lightning, and from them, flames erupt. No creature can look directly at his eyes, because anyone who tries is instantly consumed by their intense fire.

His height is so vast that it would take 2,500 years to travel its full distance. No one can fully comprehend his size, and no words can describe his great strength—only the King of kings, the Holy One, blessed be He, knows the full extent of his power.

Why is he called 'Ophanniel? Because he is in charge of the 'Ophannim, and they have been placed under his care. Every day, he stands to serve them. He enhances their beauty, organizes their chambers, polishes their foundations, refines their dwellings, smooths their edges, and cleanses their seats. He tends to them day and night, making sure they shine with splendor, stand with dignity, and are always prepared to offer praise to their Creator.

The 'Ophannim are covered in countless eyes, and their radiance shines in every direction. On the right side of their garments, seventy-two sapphire stones are placed, and another seventy-two sapphire stones decorate the left side.

Each 'Ophan wears a crown set with four glowing carbuncle stones. These stones shine in all four directions of the highest heaven, just as the light of the sun spreads across the entire universe. Why are they called carbuncle stones? Because their brilliance resembles flashing lightning.

The 'Ophannim are surrounded by magnificent tents made of sapphire and carbuncle, glowing with splendor and brilliance. These tents shield them and intensify the dazzling beauty of their shining eyes, filling the space around them with an unmatched, radiant glow."

Chapter XXV

Seraphiel, the Prince of the Seraphim

Rabbi Ishmael said: Metatron, the angel and Prince of the Presence, explained to me:

"Above all these beings stands a powerful and magnificent prince. He is extraordinary in every way—great, noble, honored, mighty, and awe-inspiring. He leads the heavenly hosts, moves with incredible speed, and is a scribe of unmatched skill. He is glorified, deeply respected, and loved by all.

His entire being radiates with splendor, shining with light and brilliance. Every part of him reflects beauty and greatness.

His face glows like that of angels, but his body is shaped like a mighty eagle.

His radiance flashes like lightning, his appearance burns like fire, and his beauty shines like the brightest stars. His glory glows like burning coals, his majesty sparkles like polished metal, and his brilliance resembles the glow of the planet Venus. His form reflects the light of the sun, and his height reaches the full span of the seven heavens. The light from his eyebrows is seven times brighter than normal light.

A massive sapphire stone rests on his head, as large as the entire universe, shining as brilliantly as the heavens themselves.

His entire body is covered with countless eyes, as numerous as the stars in the sky. Each eye shines like Venus, though some glow like the moon and others like the sun. Different parts of his body radiate different types of light:

- From his ankles to his knees, his glow is like flashing stars.
- From his knees to his thighs, it shines like Venus.
- From his thighs to his waist, it mirrors the brightness of the moon.
- From his waist to his neck, it radiates like the sun.
- From his neck to his head, it shines with a light that never fades.

The crown on his head is as brilliant as the Throne of Glory itself. Its size covers a distance that would take 200 years to travel. Upon this crown rests every kind of radiance, glow, and brilliance found in the universe.

This prince's name is Seraphiel, and the crown he wears is called the Prince of Peace. He is named Seraphiel because he is in charge of the Seraphim, the fiery beings under his care. Day and night, he watches over them, teaches them songs of praise, and guides them in exalting the beauty, power, and majesty of the King. He helps them sanctify His name with the greatest reverence.

The Seraphim are four in number, representing the four winds of the world. Each one has six wings, symbolizing the six days of Creation. They each have four faces.

Their size is beyond imagination—each Seraph is as tall as the seven heavens combined. Each wing is as wide as the entire sky, and each face is as vast as the whole eastern horizon.

The Seraphim shine with a light so intense that it rivals the brightness of the Throne of Glory. Their glow is so overwhelming that even the Holy Chayyoth, the mighty Ophannim, and the majestic Kerubim cannot look at them. Anyone who dares to gaze at them is instantly blinded by their incredible brilliance.

They are called Seraphim because they burn (saraph) the writing tables of Satan. Each day, Satan, along with Sammael, the Prince of Rome, and Dubbiel, the Prince of Persia, writes down the sins of Israel on tablets. These records are handed over to the Seraphim to present before the Holy One, blessed be He, in an attempt to accuse Israel.

But the Seraphim, knowing the hidden will of the Holy One, blessed be He, understand that He does not desire Israel's destruction. So what do they do? Every day, they take Satan's records and burn them in the flames that blaze before the Throne of Glory. By doing this, they ensure that these accusations never reach the Holy One, especially when He sits upon the Throne of Judgment to judge the world in truth."

Chapter XXVI

Radweriel, the Keeper of the Book of Records

Rabbi Ishmael said: Metatron, the Angel of the Lord and Prince of the Presence, explained to me:

"Above the Seraphim stands a prince of incredible greatness, higher than all other princes and more wondrous than any other heavenly being. His name is Radweriel, and he is responsible for guarding the treasuries of the sacred books.

Radweriel's main duty is to bring forth the Case of Writings, which holds the Book of Records. He retrieves this case and presents it before the Holy One, blessed be He. Once there, he breaks its seals, carefully opens it, and takes out the books inside. These sacred writings are then placed before the Holy One, blessed be He.

The Holy One, blessed be He, receives the books from Radweriel's hands and gives them to the heavenly scribes, whose job is to read them. This takes place in the Great Beth Din, the divine court in the highest heaven, in front of the entire heavenly assembly.

Why is he called Radweriel? His name reflects a unique and amazing ability—every word that comes from his mouth creates an angel. These angels are formed by the power of his voice and immediately join the ranks of the ministering angels, becoming part of the heavenly choirs.

When the time comes for the Thrice Holy song to be sung, Radweriel takes his place among the singing angels. He lifts his voice in praise, joining the celestial hosts as they glorify their Creator together."

Chapter XXVII

Description of a class of angels

Rabbi Ishmael said: Metatron, the Angel, the Prince of the Presence, explained to me:

Each angel is given seventy names, matching the seventy languages spoken throughout the world. All of these names come from the holy and exalted name of the Holy One, blessed be He. Every name is engraved in fire on the Fearful Crown, which rests upon the head of the high and glorious King.

From each name inscribed on this crown, sparks and flashes of lightning burst forth, filling the heavens with brilliant light. Surrounding each angel are majestic horns of splendor, forming a magnificent display around them. From these horns, streams of light shine outward, creating an endless glow.

Each angel is wrapped in tents of shimmering brightness, their light so intense and overwhelming that even the powerful Seraphim and mighty Chayyoth—greater than all other heavenly beings—cannot look at them. The radiance surrounding these angels is beyond imagination, a reflection of the infinite majesty of the Holy One, blessed be He, from whom their light and strength flow.

Chapter XXVIII

The 'Irin and Qaddishin

Rabbi Ishmael said: Metatron, the Angel, the Prince of the Presence, explained to me:

Above all the heavenly beings stand four great princes, known as the 'Irin and Qaddishin. These princes are highly honored, deeply respected, beloved, and full of glory. They are greater than all other heavenly beings, and no other celestial rulers or servants can compare to them. Each of these four princes is as powerful as all the others combined.

Their dwelling place is directly across from the Throne of Glory, and they stand before the Holy One, blessed be He. The brilliance of their presence reflects the light of the Throne of Glory, and their splendor mirrors the radiance of the Divine Presence.

They are glorified by the majesty of the Divine and praised in the light of the Shekina.

Not only are they deeply revered, but the Holy One, blessed be He, does nothing in the world without first consulting them. Only after seeking their guidance does He act, as it is written in Daniel 4:7: "The sentence is by the decree of the 'Irin and the demand by the word of the Qaddishin."

There are two 'Irin and two Qaddishin. How do they stand before the Holy One, blessed be He? One 'Ir stands on one side, and the other on the opposite side. Likewise, one Qaddish stands on one side, and the other on the opposite side.

These powerful princes lift up the humble and bring down the proud. They raise those who are lowly to great heights and humble the arrogant, lowering them to the dust.

Each day, when the Holy One, blessed be He, sits on the Throne of Judgment to judge the entire world, the Books of the Living and the Books of the Dead are opened before Him. All the heavenly beings stand in fear, awe, and trembling. As He sits upon the Throne of Judgment, His garments shine as white as snow, the hair on His head is as pure as wool, and His entire cloak glows with radiant light. His righteousness covers Him like armor.

The 'Irin and Qaddishin stand before Him like court officers before a judge. They bring cases forward, debate the issues, and bring each matter to a close before the Holy One, blessed be He, as it is written in Daniel 4:17: "The sentence is by the decree of the 'Irin and the demand by the word of the Qaddishin."

Some of them present arguments, while others issue rulings in the Great Beth Din in the highest heaven. Some request decisions from the Divine Majesty, while others finalize the cases presented before the Most High. Others descend to earth to carry out the judgments that have been declared, as it is written in Daniel 4:13-14:

"Behold, an 'Ir and a Qaddish came down from heaven and cried aloud, saying: Cut down the tree and remove its branches, shake off its leaves, and scatter its fruit. Let the animals flee from beneath it, and the birds from its branches."

Why are they called 'Irin and Qaddishin? Because they purify both body and spirit with fiery discipline on the third day of judgment, as it is written in Hosea 6:2:

"After two days, He will revive us. On the third day, He will raise us up, and we shall live before Him."

Chapter XXIX

The 72 Princes of Kingdoms and the Prince of the World officiating at the Great Sanhedrin in heaven

Rabbi Ishmael said: Metatron, the angel and Prince of the Presence, explained to me:

Whenever the Great Court gathers in the highest heavens, no one in the world is allowed to speak—except for a select group of extraordinary princes who have the honor of carrying the name of the Holy One, blessed be He.

How many of these princes are there? There are seventy-two, each one representing a different kingdom on earth. Above them all stands the Prince of the World, who speaks on behalf of all creation. Every day, this great Prince pleads for the world before the Holy One, blessed be He.

This takes place at the sacred moment when the Book of Records is opened. In this book, every action in the world is written down, ready for judgment. As it is written in Daniel 7:10: "The judgment was set, and the books were opened."

At this solemn time, the seventy-two princes and the Prince of the World stand before the Holy One, offering their petitions and arguments. Their purpose is to seek balance and mercy, ensuring that divine justice is carried out with compassion in the highest court of heaven.

Chapter XXX

The attributes of Justice, Mercy, and Truth by the throne of judgment

Rabbi Ishmael said: Metatron, the angel and Prince of the Presence, explained to me:

When the Holy One, blessed be He, sits on the Throne of Judgment to make decisions, three powerful forces stand around Him. Justice is on His right, representing fairness and doing what is right. Mercy is on His left, shining with kindness and compassion. Truth stands directly in front of Him, glowing with honesty and purity.

When a person comes before Him for judgment, something remarkable happens. A staff of light emerges from the glow of Mercy and moves in front of the person. This staff is a sign that compassion is present, even in the face of judgment.

At that moment, the person falls to the ground in humility and awe. The angels of destruction, who are there to carry out punishments, tremble with fear and cannot approach because the power of Mercy is too strong.

As it is written in Isaiah 16:5: "With mercy, the throne will be established, and He will sit upon it in truth." This verse shows how justice and compassion work together on the Throne of the Holy One, blessed be He. Mercy softens judgment, ensuring that decisions are fair and true while also offering hope and redemption to those who come before Him.

Chapter XXXI

The execution of judgement on the wicked. God's sword

Rabbi Ishmael said: Metatron, the angel and Prince of the Presence, told me:

When the Holy One, blessed be He, opens the Book of Records—a divine book made of fire and flame—His judgment begins. From His presence, commands are constantly sent out, ensuring that justice is carried out against the wicked. This is done through His sword, which is drawn from its sheath.

The sword shines as brightly as lightning, and its brilliance spreads across the entire world, lighting up everything from one end of the earth to the other. As it is written in Isaiah: "For by fire, the Lord will judge, and by His sword, all flesh."

The sight of this sword fills everyone on earth with fear and trembling. Its sharp blade flashes like lightning, stretching across the horizon. Sparks and bursts of light, as bright as the stars, shoot from the sword, adding to the overwhelming power it displays. As it is written in Deuteronomy: "If I sharpen the lightning of My sword."

Chapter XXXII

When the Holy One, blessed be He, sits on the Throne of Judgment, different groups of angels take their places around Him. The angels of Mercy stand on His right, showing compassion and speaking on behalf of those being judged. On His left are the angels of Peace, radiating calm and tranquility. Directly in front of Him are the angels of Destruction, ready to carry out His commands as He sees fit.

Beneath the Throne of Glory, a scribe records everything happening in the heavenly court. Another scribe stands above the Throne, writing down the divine decrees spoken by the Holy One, blessed be He.

Surrounding the Throne on all four sides are the Seraphim, powerful beings made of fire. Their presence forms walls of light and flames that enclose the divine seat. The Ophannim also encircle the Throne, their fiery bodies covered in flames that shine in all directions. To the right and left of the Throne, there are clouds of fire, adding to the incredible majesty of the scene.

Beneath the Throne, the Holy Chayyoth carry it, each with three enormous fingers. The size of each finger is immense, measuring 800,000 and 70 times 100, plus 66,000 parasangs. These mighty beings stand in a breathtaking display of divine power, their strength holding up the Throne of Glory.

Under the feet of the Chayyoth, seven fiery rivers flow endlessly. Each river stretches 3,500 thousand parasangs wide and plunges 248 thousand myriads of parasangs deep. Their length is beyond comprehension, impossible to measure. These rivers curve and flow in all four directions of Araboth, their power spreading across the heavens.

From Araboth, the rivers descend to Mâ'ân, where they pause before moving on to Zebul, then to Shechagim, then to Raqia', and finally to Shamayim. From there, the rivers pour down upon the heads of the wicked in Gehenna, delivering divine judgment. As it is written in Jeremiah 33:19:

"Behold, a whirlwind of the Lord, even His fury, has gone forth, a whirling tempest; it shall burst upon the head of the wicked."

Chapter XXXIII

Rabbi Ishmael said: Metatron, the angel and Prince of the Presence, explained to me:

The feet of the Chayyoth are surrounded by seven layers of burning coals, each glowing with intense heat. Beyond these coals are seven walls of fire, their flames flickering and lighting up everything around them.

Outside these fiery walls are seven layers of hailstones, known as the stones of 'Elgabish, as described in Ezekiel. These hailstones shine with an icy glow, creating a sharp contrast to the fire within. Surrounding them is another layer of hailstones, called the stones of Bârâd, adding yet another powerful barrier.

Beyond these stones are layers of stormy winds, known as the wings of the tempest, swirling with uncontrollable energy. Further out, layers of flames roar fiercely, consuming everything in their path.

These flames are surrounded by the chambers of the whirlwind, constantly spinning and churning. Beyond these chambers are the realms of fire and water, two opposing elements that exist together in perfect balance, sustained by divine power.

Encircling the realms of fire and water are angels

who never stop proclaiming "Holy!" as they lift their voices in praise. Beyond them are those who chant "Blessed!" in perfect harmony, their voices echoing throughout the heavens.

Surrounding the singers of "Blessed!" are glowing clouds, radiant with divine light. These clouds are enclosed by burning juniper coals, their heat intense and unrelenting. Around the juniper coals are a thousand camps of fire and ten thousand hosts of flames, each burning with incredible brightness.

Between each camp and host lies a protective cloud, shielding the heavenly beings from the overwhelming fire. These clouds act as a divine barrier, allowing the angels to fulfill their sacred duties and continue their endless worship of the Holy One, blessed be He.

Chapter XXXIV

Rabbi Ishmael said: The angel Metatron, the Prince of the Presence, explained to me:

In the highest heaven, called Araboth Raqia', God created an enormous number of angels—506,000 groups in total. Each group has 49,000 angels, and they are incredibly powerful and awe-inspiring.

Each angel is as vast as the ocean. Their faces shine as bright as lightning, their eyes glow like fire, and their arms and legs gleam like polished metal. When they speak, their voices boom like a mighty roar, full of strength and majesty.

All of these angels stand before God's Throne of Glory in four enormous rows. Each row is led by powerful angelic commanders who guide them with authority and dedication.

Some angels spend their time calling out "Holy!" while others say "Blessed!" Some act as swift messengers, rushing to carry out God's commands, while others remain still, standing in deep respect before Him. As it says in the Book of Daniel:

"Thousands upon thousands served Him, and ten thousand times ten thousand stood before Him. The court was seated, and the books were opened."

When it is time to declare the Kedushsha—the sacred praise of God—a great whirlwind suddenly bursts forth from before Him. This storm moves through the Camp of Shekhinah, shaking the heavens, just as it is written in Jeremiah:

"Look! The whirlwind of the Lord goes out in fury, a raging storm."

In that moment, thousands of angels transform into flashes of fire, streaks of lightning, and bursts of energy. Some turn into flames, rushing winds, or blazing fires. Others take the shape of glowing figures, shining like living sparks of light.

These changes happen because they fully submit to God's power. They tremble with awe and fear, overwhelmed by His presence.

They stay in this state of intense motion and energy until they completely embrace their purpose—to praise the glorious King. Once they do, they return to their original forms, standing strong and devoted. Their focus never shifts from singing praises to God, just as it says in Isaiah:

"And one called to another and said: Holy, Holy, Holy is the Lord of Hosts; the whole earth is filled with His glory."

Chapter XXXV

The angels bathe in the fiery river before reciting the Song

Rabbi Ishmael said: Metatron, the Angel, the Prince of the Presence, explained to me:

When the angels get ready to sing their Song of Praise, a powerful river of fire, called Nehar diNur, rises up, glowing with intense energy. This blazing river is filled with countless angels, each radiating strength and divine fire. It flows beneath God's Throne of Glory, passing between the angels' camps and the vast ranks of 'Araboth.

Before they can begin their song, the angels must first enter this fiery river. Each one fully immerses themselves in the flames, cleansing their spirit and preparing for the sacred task ahead. They dip their entire bodies into the fire, then carefully purify their tongues and mouths seven times, making sure their words are worthy of being offered to God.

Once purified, they emerge from the river and dress in shining robes of Machage Samal, glowing with purity and beauty. Over these, they wrap themselves in shimmering cloaks of chashmal, radiating divine light.

Clothed in this sacred attire, they take their places in four perfect rows before the Throne of Glory.

This holy gathering stretches across all the heavens, with every angel standing ready to sing. In their purified state, they reflect the greatness and holiness of their Creator, prepared to lift their voices in perfect harmony to praise Him.

Chapter XXXVI

The four camps of Shekina and their surroundings

Rabbi Ishmael said: The angel Metatron, the Prince of the Presence, explained to me:

Inside the seven heavenly halls, there are four magnificent chariots of Shekina, each shining with divine glory. In front of every chariot stand four great groups of Shekina's celestial army, filled with unmatched beauty and holiness. Flowing between these groups is a mighty river of fire, burning endlessly, symbolizing the eternal power of God's presence.

Surrounding the fiery rivers are glowing clouds, casting a soft, sacred light across the heavens. Between these clouds rise towering pillars of brimstone, standing strong as symbols of divine power and purity. Around each pillar, flaming wheels spin in endless motion, forming brilliant circles of fire.

Between these fiery wheels, flames blaze continuously, never fading. Within these flames are great treasuries of lightning, bursting with dazzling flashes that light up the heavens with awe. Beyond the lightning are the mighty wings of the storm wind, always moving, carrying out God's will across the universe.

Behind these powerful winds are the chambers of the storm, where the wild forces of nature gather and are held in place. Beyond these chambers lie vast realms filled with roaring winds, echoing voices, rolling thunder, and endless bursts of sparks. Layer upon layer, earthquakes rumble behind them, shaking one after another, their force revealing the unshakable power of the Holy One.

This breathtaking and intricate arrangement reflects divine order, with each element playing its role in upholding the chariots and the heavenly hosts of Shekina—eternal signs of God's infinite glory and rule.

Chapter XXXVII

The fear that befalls all the heavens at the sound of the Holy, especially the heavenly bodies, and their appeasement by the Prince of the World

Rabbi Ishmael said: The angel Metatron, the Prince of the Presence, explained to me:

Within the seven heavenly halls, there are four majestic chariots of Shekina, each glowing with divine light. In front of these chariots stand four great groups of Shekina's celestial army, filled with beauty and holiness beyond imagination. Flowing between these groups is a powerful river of fire, burning without end, representing the everlasting presence of God.

Surrounding this fiery river are bright, glowing clouds that spread a soft, sacred light. Between them rise towering pillars of brimstone, standing firm as symbols of divine strength and purity. Around each pillar, spinning wheels of fire create endless, dazzling circles of light.

Between these fiery wheels, flames burn without stopping. Inside these flames are great stores of lightning, sending out brilliant flashes that fill the heavens with awe. Beyond the lightning, the mighty wings of the storm winds move without rest, carrying out God's will across creation.

Behind these powerful winds are the chambers of the storm, where the forces of nature are gathered and held. Beyond them stretch vast realms filled with rushing winds, echoing voices, rolling thunder, and endless bursts of sparks. Layer after layer, earthquakes shake the space behind them, one trembling after another, revealing the unstoppable power of the Holy One.

This incredible and intricate structure reflects the divine order, with each part playing its role in upholding the chariots and the heavenly hosts of Shekina—eternal symbols of God's endless glory and rule.

Chapter XXXVIII

The explicit names fly off from the Throne, and all the various angelic hosts prostrate themselves before it during the Qedushsha

Rabbi Ishmael said: The angel Metatron, the Prince of the Presence, explained to me:

When the angels begin to chant "Holy," something incredible happens. The sacred names of God, written in fiery letters on the Throne of Glory, suddenly take flight. These powerful names rise into the sky like mighty eagles, each one shining with divine energy. They are carried by sixteen wings and soar together, circling around the Holy One on all sides of His divine presence.

As this sacred moment unfolds, all the angels and heavenly beings watch in awe. The radiant angels join with the fiery Servants, the powerful Ophannim, and the Kerubim of Shekina. The shining Chayyoth stand alongside the Seraphim, the 'Er'ellim, and the Mephsarim. Armies of fire, blazing with intense flames, gather in deep worship.

The holy princes, wearing crowns of glory, stand in robes that shine like royal garments. Their very beings radiate strength and splendor. In complete humility, they bow before God, lowering themselves three times in perfect harmony.

Their voices rise together, filling the heavens with a powerful declaration: "Blessed be the name of His glorious kingdom forever and ever." Their worship reflects the unity of creation, the purpose of their existence, and their deep reverence for the One who rules over all.

Chapter XXXIX

The ministering angels rewarded with crowns for properly uttering the "Holy," and consumed by fire for failing, with new ones created to take their place

Rabbi Ishmael said: The angel Metatron, the Prince of the Presence, explained to me:

When the angels chant "Holy" before God with the right order and deep respect, a moment of divine joy fills the heavens. The attendants of His Throne of Glory step forward, emerging with great happiness. Each of them carries countless crowns—thousands upon thousands, shining brightly like the planet Venus.

These crowns are given to the angels and the great heavenly princes who proclaim "Holy." Each one receives three crowns: the first for saying "Holy," the second for saying "Holy, Holy," and the third for completing the chant with "Holy, Holy, Holy is the Lord of Hosts." This act shows God's approval and pleasure, recognizing their devotion and place in the heavenly order.

However, if the angels fail to say "Holy" in the correct way or without proper focus, a blazing fire bursts from the little finger of God. This fire rushes into their ranks, splitting into 496,000 flames, each one directed at the four great camps of the angels. In a single moment, those who made mistakes are consumed by the flames, as it is written: "A fire goes before Him and burns up His enemies all around."

But immediately after, God speaks a single word, and from that word, new angels are created to take the place of those who were lost. These newly formed angels stand before the Throne of Glory and join in the never-ending song of praise, declaring "Holy" without hesitation. As it is written: "They are new every morning; great is Your faithfulness." Each day, fresh and renewed angels rise to continue the eternal worship of God.

Chapter XL

Metatron shows R. Ishmael the letters engraved on the Throne of Glory, by which all of creation was made

R. Ishmael said: Metatron, the Angel, the Prince of the Presence, spoke to me and said:

Come and see the letters that shaped the heavens and the earth—the same letters that formed the mountains and hills. These are the letters that created the seas and rivers, the trees, and every plant that grows on the land. They are the letters that brought the planets and stars into existence, setting the sun, moon, and great constellations like Orion and the Pleiades into their places, filling the sky with light.

These same letters were used to create the Throne of Glory, the spinning Wheels of the Merkaba, and everything needed to sustain the universe. Through them, wisdom, understanding, and knowledge came to be. They also formed virtues like patience, humility, and righteousness, which keep the world in balance.

As I walked beside him, he held my hand and lifted me onto his wings. He showed me these sacred letters, each one carved in flames upon the Throne of Glory. Sparks flew from them, their light spreading out and filling all the chambers of 'Araboth, shining across the highest heavens with their brilliance.

Chapter XLI

R. Ishmael said: Metatron, the Angel, the Prince of the Presence, said to me:

Come, and I will show you where amazing things happen. I will take you to the place where water is suspended high above, where fire burns inside hail but is never put out, where lightning flashes from snowy mountains, where thunder echoes in the highest heavens, where flames burn inside other flames, and where powerful voices sound through thunder and earthquakes.

As we walked, he took my hand and lifted me onto his wings, showing me all these wonders. I saw the waters held high in 'Araboth Raqia', kept in place by the power of the name YAH 'EHYEH ASHER 'EHYEH (I Am That I Am). From these waters, streams flowed down to the earth, nourishing it, just as it is written: "He waters the mountains from His chambers; the earth is satisfied with the fruit of His works."

I also saw fire and snow side by side, neither harming the other, kept in perfect balance by the power of the name 'ESHK 'OKLA (Consuming Fire), as it is written: "For the Lord your God is a consuming fire."

I watched as flashes of lightning shot out from snowy mountains, yet they did not fade, sustained by the power of the name YAH TSUR OLAMIM (The Everlasting Rock), as it is written: "For in Jah, the Lord, is an everlasting rock."

I heard roaring thunder and mighty voices rising from fiery flames, their sound never fading, held strong by the power of the name 'EL SHADDAI RABBA (The Great God Almighty), as it is written: "I am God Almighty."

I saw flames glowing brightly inside other flames, burning without being consumed, upheld by the power of the name CAD AL KES YAH (The Hand Upon the Throne of the Lord), as it is written: "For the hand is upon the Throne of the Lord."

I witnessed rivers of fire flowing alongside rivers of water, yet neither one destroyed the other. They remained in harmony through the power of the name OSEH SHALOM (Maker of Peace), as it is written: "He makes peace in His high places." For it is He who creates peace between fire and water, hail and flame, wind and cloud, earthquake and sparks.

Chapter XLII

Metatron shows R. Ishmael the abode of the unborn spirits and of the spirits of the righteous dead

R. Ishmael said: Metatron said to me:

"Come, and I will show you where the spirits of the righteous are—those who have already lived and returned, as well as those who have not yet been born."

He brought me close, took my hand, and lifted me up near the Throne of Glory, the place where the Shekina dwells. There, he revealed the Throne of Glory to me, and I saw the spirits that had lived and returned. They were soaring above the throne, in the presence of the Holy One.

Then, I reflected on a verse from Scripture and found its meaning in what is written: "For the spirit clothed itself before me, and the souls I have made" (Isaiah 57:16). The words "for the spirit clothed itself before me" refer to the spirits that were created in the chamber of creation for the righteous and have returned to God. The phrase "the souls I have made" refers to the spirits of the righteous who have not yet been born and remain in a chamber known as GUPH.

Chapter XLIII

Metatron shows R. Ishmael the abode of the wicked and the intermediate in Sheol. (vss. 1–6)

The Patriarchs pray for the deliverance of Israel (vss. 7–10)

R. Ishmael said: Metatron, the Angel, the Prince of the Presence, said to me:

"Come, and I will show you where the spirits of the wicked and those in between dwell, where they stand, and where they are taken. I will show you where the in-between spirits descend and where the wicked are cast down."

He said to me, "Two angels of destruction, Za'aphiel and Simkiel, send the spirits of the wicked to Sheol."

Simkiel is responsible for the in-between spirits, guiding and purifying them because of the great mercy of Adonai, the Prince of the Place. Za'aphiel is in charge of the wicked, driving them away from God's presence and the splendor of the Shekina. They are sent to Sheol to be punished in the fire of Gehenna, beaten with rods of burning coal.

As we walked, he took my hand and pointed out everything with his fingers.

I saw their faces—they looked human, but their bodies were like eagles. The spirits of those in between had a pale grey appearance because of their actions. Their sins left marks on them until they were cleansed by fire.

The faces of the wicked, however, were as black as the bottom of a pot, showing the depth of their evil and the wrongs they had done.

Then I saw the spirits of the Patriarchs—Abraham, Isaac, and Jacob—along with the spirits of the righteous. They had risen from their graves and ascended to the Heaven of Raqia'. Standing before God, they prayed with sorrow in their voices:

"Lord of the Universe, how much longer will You remain on Your Throne in mourning, with Your right hand held back? When will You rescue Your children and reveal Your Kingdom to the world? How much longer will You leave Your people as slaves among the nations? When will You show mercy once more? The hand with which You stretched out the heavens and the earth—when will You raise it again in compassion?"

God answered them, saying, "How can I act while the wicked continue to sin so terribly? How can I lift My mighty right hand when their wrongdoing has caused such destruction?"

At that moment, Metatron turned to me and said, "My servant, take the books and read their deeds!" I took the books and read the records of their actions. Every wicked soul had broken the Torah in every possible way, disobeying every law and commandment. As it is written, "Yes, all Israel has transgressed Your Law" (Daniel 9:11). The word was not written as toratecha but torateka, meaning they had violated every letter of the Torah, from the first (Aleph) to the last (Tav). Each letter of the Torah stood as a witness against them.

Upon hearing this, Abraham, Isaac, and Jacob wept bitterly. Then God said to them, "Abraham, My beloved; Isaac, My chosen one; Jacob, My firstborn— how can I now rescue these people from the hands of the nations?"

At that moment, Mihmael, the Prince of Israel, cried out in grief, weeping loudly, and said, "Why do You stand far off, O Lord?" (Psalm 10:1).

Chapter XLIV

Metatron shows R. Ishmael last and future events recorded on the Curtain of the Throne

R. Ishmael said: Metatron said to me:

"Come, and I will show you the Curtain of MAQOM, where the Divine Majesty is displayed. On it, every generation of the world is recorded—all their actions, past and future, until the end of time."

He took me with him, pointing things out with his fingers, like a father teaching his child to read the Torah. I saw every generation and its leaders:

- The rulers and heads of each generation
- The guides and shepherds
- The oppressors and those in power
- The protectors and guardians
- The judges and court officials
- The teachers and supporters
- The noblemen and warriors
- The elders and counselors

I saw Adam and his generation, their deeds and thoughts.

I saw Noah and his generation, their choices and actions.

I saw those who lived before the flood, their behavior and their fate.

I saw Shem and Nimrod, and the generation of the Tower of Babel, their struggles and their beliefs.

I saw Abraham, Isaac, and Ishmael—each with their own generation and their deeds.

I saw Jacob, Joseph, and the twelve tribes, their lives and their journeys.

I saw Moses and his people, Aaron, Miriam, the elders, and the leaders of Israel.

Then Metatron spoke:

"I saw Joshua and his generation, their victories and failures.

I saw the judges of Israel, their wisdom and struggles.

I saw Eli, Phinehas, and Samuel, and how they led their people.

I saw the kings of Judah and Israel, the choices they made, and their impact on history.

I saw the princes of Israel and the rulers of other nations, their ambitions and their deeds.

I saw the heads of councils in Israel and the nations, their leadership and decisions.

I saw the nobles, the judges, and the wise men— both of Israel and the other nations.

I saw the teachers of children in Israel and across the world, shaping the next generations.

I saw the prophets of Israel and the prophets of the nations, their messages and warnings.

I witnessed every war and battle that the nations fought against Israel during its time as a kingdom.

I saw the Messiah, the son of Joseph, and his generation, their actions, and their struggles against the nations.

I saw the Messiah, the son of David, and his time— his battles, his triumphs, and his hardships alongside Israel.

I saw the great wars of Gog and Magog in the days of the Messiah, and everything that God will do in those times.

I saw every leader, every generation, and every event—both in Israel and among the nations. Everything that has happened and everything that will take place until the end of time was written on the Curtain of MAQOM.

I saw it all with my own eyes. After witnessing these things, I opened my mouth to praise MAQOM, saying:

"For the King's word has power, and who may say to Him, 'What are You doing?'" (Ecclesiastes 8:4).

"O Lord, how great are Your works!" (Psalm 104:24).

Chapter XLV

The place of the stars shown to R. Ishmael

R. Ishmael said: Metatron said to me:

"Come, and I will show you where the stars rest, where they stand each night in the sky, filled with awe for MAQOM, and where they move from their places of rest."

I walked beside him as he took my hand, pointing out everything with his fingers. I saw the stars standing on sparks of blazing fire, surrounding the Chariot of the Almighty. Then Metatron clapped his hands, and the stars were set into motion. Instantly, they shot into the sky on fiery wings, scattering in all directions from the Throne of the Merkaba. As they soared, Metatron spoke the name of each one to me, fulfilling what is written: "He counts the number of the stars; He gives each one its name" (Psalm 147:4). This shows that the Holy One has given every star a unique name.

With perfect order, each star follows Haniel into the heavens, Raqia' hashamayim, to serve the world. When their task is done, they return in the same way to sing praises to the Holy One through songs and hymns, as it is written: "The heavens declare the glory of God"

(Psalm 19:1).

In the future, the Holy One will make them new again, as it is written: "They are new every morning" (Lamentations 3:23). Then, they will open their mouths to sing a song of praise. What will they sing? It is written: "When I consider Your heavens..." (Psalm 8:3).

Chapter XLVI

Metatron shows R. Ishmael the spirits of the punished angels

R. Ishmael said: Metatron said to me:

"Come, and I will show you the souls of the angels and the spirits of the heavenly servants whose bodies have been burned by the fire of MAQOM (the Almighty). This fire comes from His little finger. These angels have been turned into fiery coals within the River of Fire (Nehar diNur), but their spirits and souls remain behind the Shekina, standing in eternal reverence.

Whenever the heavenly servants sing at the wrong time or in a way that was not commanded, they are consumed by the fire of their Creator. A flame sent by God burns them up within the chambers of the whirlwind. This mighty wind sweeps them away, casting them into the River of Fire, where they are transformed into great mountains of burning coal. However, their spirits and souls always return to their Creator, continuing to stand behind Him in devotion.

I walked beside Metatron as he took my hand and led me to see these spirits and souls. He showed me where they stood behind the Shekina, resting on the wings of the whirlwind and surrounded by walls of fire.

Then Metatron opened the gates of the fiery walls where these spirits remained behind the Shekina. I looked up and saw them. They had the forms of angels, and their wings were like those of birds, but made entirely of flames, created from burning fire.

In that moment, I opened my mouth and praised MAQOM, saying: 'How great are Your works, O Lord!' (Psalm 92:3)."

Chapter XLVII (A)

Metatron shows R. Ishmael the Right Hand of the Most High, now inactive behind Him, but in the future destined to work the deliverance of Israel

R. Ishmael said: Metatron said to me:

"Come, and I will show you the Right Hand of MAQOM, which has been placed behind Him since the destruction of the Holy Temple. From it shines every kind of light and splendor, and through it, the 955 heavens were created. Even the seraphim and Ophannim are not allowed to look at it until the day of salvation arrives.

I walked beside him, and he took my hand. With joy, songs, and praise, he showed me the Right Hand of MAQOM. No words can fully describe its beauty, and no eyes can withstand its greatness, majesty, and glory.

By its side stand the souls of the righteous, those found worthy to witness the joy of Jerusalem. They praise and pray before it three times a day, saying, "Awake, awake, put on strength, O arm of the Lord." As it is written: "He caused His glorious arm to go at the right hand of Moses."

At that moment, the Right Hand of MAQOM was weeping. From its five fingers, five rivers of tears flowed down into the great sea, shaking the entire world. This is as written in Scripture: "The earth is utterly broken, the earth is torn apart, the earth shakes violently. The earth will stagger like a drunken man and sway like a hut." These five events are connected to the five fingers of His mighty hand.

When the Holy One sees that there is no righteous person left in the generation, no one devoted to goodness, and no justice among people—when there is no one like Moses or Samuel to stand before Him and pray for salvation and deliverance—when no one calls upon His Right Hand to act on behalf of Israel, then He remembers His own justice, mercy, and grace. By His own power, He will bring salvation. As it is written:

"He saw that there was no one, and He was amazed that there was no one to intercede; so His own arm brought salvation, and His righteousness upheld Him."

Scripture reminds us how Moses constantly prayed for Israel in the wilderness, preventing divine judgment, and how Samuel called upon God, who answered his prayers, even when they were not part of the divine plan. As it is written: "Moses and Aaron were among His priests" and "Even if Moses and Samuel stood before Me."

At that time, the Holy One will say: "How long shall I wait for humanity to bring salvation through their righteousness? For My own sake, for My merit and justice, I will stretch out My arm and redeem My children from among the nations." As it is written: "For My own sake I will do it, for how can My name be defiled?"

Then the Holy One will reveal His mighty arm to the nations. It will stretch across the whole world, shining with the brilliance of the summer sun at its peak.

In that moment, Israel will be saved from the nations. The Messiah will appear and lead them to Jerusalem with great joy. They will feast and celebrate, glorifying the Messianic Kingdom and the house of David throughout the world. No nation will have power over them anymore. The people of Israel will gather from the four corners of the earth and dine with the Messiah. But the nations of the world will not share in their feast, as it is written:

"The Lord has bared His holy arm in the sight of all the nations, and all the ends of the earth shall see the salvation of our God."

And again: "The Lord alone led him, and there was no foreign god with him."

"And the Lord shall be King over all the earth."

Chapter XLVII (B)

The Divine Flames that go forth from the Throne of Glory, crowned and escorted by numerous angelic hosts through the heavens and back again to the Throne—the angels sing the Holy and the Blessed

Metatron said to me:

These are the seventy-two sacred names that are written upon the heart of the Holy One. They are names of power, righteousness, and majesty: SeDeQ, SaHPeL, SUR, SaDdiQ, SeBa'oTh (Lord of Hosts), ShaDdaY (God Almighty), 'eLoHIM (God), YHWH, and many others of great holiness. Among them are names like ROKeB 'aRaBOTh (He who rides upon the Araboth), HaY (The Living One), and QQQ (Holy, Holy, Holy). Each of these names carries deep meaning and mystery, declaring His eternal glory and dominion. They affirm His strength and wisdom, as written:

"He gives power to the weary and increases strength to those who have no might."

These names are surrounded by countless crowns—crowns of fire, crowns of flame, crowns of chashmal, and crowns of lightning. They are accompanied by thousands upon thousands of powerful angels, carrying them with honor like subjects escorting a mighty king. These angelic hosts surround them with pillars of fire, glowing clouds, flashes of lightning, and brilliant light. Wherever they move, there is awe, trembling, majesty, and deep reverence, along with dignity, glory, wisdom, and understanding. Their journey is marked by the brightness of chashmal and the splendor of divine radiance.

As they travel through the heavens, these sacred names are praised. The angels call out before them, "Holy, Holy, Holy!" The heavenly hosts roll them through the realms of the skies, treating them as honored and mighty princes.

When these names are finally brought back to the Throne of Glory, the Chayyoth surrounding the Merkaba open their mouths in praise. They declare the holiness and greatness of His name, saying:

"Blessed be the Name of His glorious kingdom forever and ever."

Chapter XLVII (C)

An EnochMetatron piece

I took him, strengthened him, and gave him a special purpose. I chose Enoch, my servant, who is unlike any other among the children of heaven. I made him strong during the time of the first Adam. But when I saw how corrupt the people of the flood generation had become, I removed my Shekina from among them. I lifted it up to the heavens with the sound of a trumpet and a mighty shout, as it is written:

"God has gone up with a shout, the Lord with the sound of a trumpet."

I took Enoch, the son of Jared, from among humans and raised him up to the high heavens with the sound of a trumpet and a loud cry. I made him my witness among the Chayyoth of the Merkaba in the world to come. I gave him a throne that stands near my own Throne of Glory, measuring seventy thousand parasangs, all made of fire. I assigned him seventy angels, representing the seventy nations of the world, and gave him authority over all realms, both in heaven and on earth.

I granted him wisdom and understanding greater than all other angels. I gave him the name The Lesser Yah, a name whose Gematria value is seventy-one. I placed him in charge of the works of creation, making his power greater than that of the ministering angels.

I appointed him over all the treasuries and storage places in every heaven and gave him the keys to each one. He became the prince over all heavenly rulers, a minister of the Throne of Glory, and the overseer of the Halls of Araboth, with the authority to open their doors before me. He was given the responsibility to arrange and exalt the Throne of Glory.

I placed him over the Holy Chayyoth, crowning them with honor, and over the majestic Ophannim, strengthening them with glory. He was assigned to clothe the exalted Kerubim with majesty and make the radiant sparks shine with brilliance.

I gave him authority over the flaming Seraphim, covering them with greatness, and over the Chashmallim, filling them with radiant light. His task was to prepare my seat every morning. As the highest prince, he ensured that the Holy Chayyoth were crowned with majesty and clothed with honor, ready to carry out their divine roles.

I seated him before my Throne of Glory so that he could magnify my name in its fullness. He was entrusted with revealing my power and holding the secrets of both the heavens and the earth. He was chosen to witness my greatness as I sat upon my throne in majesty and splendor.

I made him greater than all others, raising him to a height of seventy thousand parasangs among the mighty. His throne was exalted to reflect my own, and its glory was increased to match the honor of my presence.

I transformed his body—his flesh became blazing fire, and his bones turned into burning coals. His eyes shone like flashes of lightning, and his eyebrows glowed with endless light. His face radiated like the sun, and his eyes reflected the majesty of the Throne of Glory.

I dressed him in honor and majesty, wrapping him in beauty and greatness. On his head, I placed a royal crown—a diadem of unmatched brilliance, measuring five hundred by five hundred parasangs. I adorned him with my own honor, majesty, and the splendor that shines from my Throne of Glory.

I called him The Lesser YHWH, The Prince of the Presence, and The Knower of Secrets. I revealed every mystery to him, just as a father shares knowledge with his son. I entrusted him with all secrets, ensuring that he would proclaim them in righteousness and truth.

I established his throne at the entrance to my Hall, where he sits to judge the heavenly hosts. Every prince of heaven stands before him, receiving instructions from him to carry out the will of the Most High.

Seventy names, taken from my own names, were given to him to elevate his status. I placed seventy princes under his command, ensuring they followed my words in every language.

I gave him the power to humble the proud and raise up the lowly. With a single word, he could bring down kings and redirect their paths. He was granted the authority to establish rulers in their positions, as it is written:

"He changes the times and the seasons; He removes kings and sets up kings." (Daniel 2:21)

He was tasked with giving wisdom to the wise and knowledge to those who seek understanding, as it is written:

"And He gives knowledge to those who understand." (Daniel 2:21)

He was chosen to reveal the secrets of my words and teach the laws of my righteous judgment, as it is written:

"So shall my word be that goes forth from my mouth; it shall not return to me empty but shall accomplish what I desire." (Isaiah 55:11)

The phrase "I shall accomplish" is not used, but rather "he shall accomplish", meaning that whatever command comes from the Holy One, Metatron carries it out faithfully. He upholds and establishes the decrees of the Holy One.

I entrusted him with teaching the Law, the Books of Wisdom, the Haggada, and the Tradition, ensuring that those who study them gain complete understanding. As it is written:

"Whom will He teach knowledge? And whom will He make understand tradition? Those weaned from milk, taken from the breast." (Isaiah 28:9)

Chapter XLVII (D)

Metatron has seventy names, which the Holy One took from His own name and gave to him to increase his glory. These names include Yehoel Yah, Yehoel, Yophiel, Aphphiel, Margziel, Simkam, Yahseyah, Ssbibyah, Periel, TatrieI, Tabkiel, and many others. Each name reflects the divine power and holiness given to him. One of these names is The Lesser YHWH, because God's own name is within him, as it is written:

"For My name is in him." (Exodus 23:21)

Another name, Sagnesakiel, refers to his role as the guardian of all the treasuries of wisdom.

All the knowledge of wisdom was entrusted to Metatron, and it was through him that this wisdom was revealed to Moses on Mount Sinai. During the forty days Moses stayed on the mountain, he learned the Torah in seventy forms and seventy languages. He also studied the Prophets, Writings, Halakhas (laws), Traditions, Haggadas, and Toseftas, all in seventy forms and languages. This covered every aspect of divine knowledge and law. However, at the end of the forty days, Moses forgot everything he had learned in an instant.

Then the Holy One called Yephiphyah, the Prince of the Law, and through him, all the knowledge was restored to Moses as a gift. As it is written:

"And the Lord gave them unto me." (Deuteronomy 10:4)

From that moment on, the knowledge remained with Moses forever. And how do we know this? It is written:

"Remember the Law of Moses, My servant, which I commanded him at Horeb for all Israel—My statutes and judgments." (Malachi 4:4)

Here, "the Law of Moses" refers to the Torah, Prophets, and Writings. "Statutes" refer to the Halakhas and Traditions, and "Judgments" refer to the Haggadas and Toseftas. All of this sacred knowledge and wisdom was given to Moses directly from the heavens on Mount Sinai.

The seventy names given to Metatron reflect the Explicit Names engraved on the Merkaba and the Throne of Glory. These sacred names were taken from God's own names and placed upon Metatron. The ministering angels use these seventy names to address the King of Kings in the highest heavens. Alongside these names, there are also twenty-two letters engraved on the ring of His finger. This ring is used to seal the destinies of the heavenly rulers, the Angel of Death, and the fate of every nation on earth.

Metatron is known as the Angel, the Prince of the Presence, and the Prince of Wisdom, Understanding, Kings, Rulers, and Glory. He was honored above all the great beings of heaven and earth. He himself testified, saying:

"The God of Israel is my witness that when I revealed this great secret to Moses, all the heavenly hosts rose up against me in outrage."

The angels demanded to know why such sacred knowledge—the very secret by which the heavens, the earth, the seas, the mountains, the rivers, Gehenna, the Garden of Eden, the Tree of Life, and even the Torah itself were created—was given to a mortal man.

"Why would you share this with someone born of a woman, a being made of flesh, imperfect and unclean? Did you get permission from the heavens? Were you granted authority from the Holy Place?"

In response, Metatron declared that the Holy One had indeed given him the authority and permission to reveal these secrets. But the angels were still not satisfied until God Himself stepped in. He rebuked them and said:

"I delight in Metatron, my servant. I have chosen him, loved him, and entrusted him with these mysteries.

He is unique among all the children of heaven."

With God's approval, Metatron took these treasures of wisdom and revealed them to Moses. Moses then passed them on to Joshua, who gave them to the elders. The elders then passed them down to the prophets, and from the prophets, they were entrusted to the men of the Great Synagogue.

From there, they were handed to Ezra the Scribe, then to Hillel the Elder, and later to R. Abbahu, who passed them to R. Zera. R. Zera then entrusted them to the men of faith, whose role was to use this knowledge to guide, warn, and heal all the diseases afflicting the world.

As it is written:

"If you listen carefully to the voice of the Lord your God, do what is right in His eyes, pay attention to His commands, and keep all His laws, I will not bring upon you any of the diseases I brought upon Egypt, for I am the Lord who heals you." (Exodus 15:26)

And so, this sacred wisdom was passed down through the generations, preserving the knowledge and healing power entrusted by the Creator of the World.

(Ended and finished. Praise be to the Creator of the World.)

Thank You for Reading

Dear Reader,

We hope this timeless classic has sparked your imagination and enriched your literary journey. Now that you've turned the final page, we want to share a vision for the future of reading—one where every classic you've ever wanted to explore is at your fingertips, in a format that best suits your life.

We'd like to invite you to gain immediate, unlimited digital & audiobook access to hundreds of the most treasured literary classics ever written—along with the option to secure deluxe paperback, hardcover & box set editions at printing cost. Together, we can spark a new global literary renaissance alongside our small, independent publishing house called "The Library of Alexandria."

Thousands of years ago, the Library of Alexandria stood as a beacon of knowledge—until it was lost to history. We aim to reignite that spirit of preservation and discovery right now, in the modern age—only this time, it's accessible to all, in every language and every format.

Picture a world where every timeless classic, novel, poem, or philosophical treatise is not only available to read but also updated for today's readers—modernized, translated into any language or dialect, and ready to enjoy in any format you choose, whether that is in an eBook, audiobook, paperback, or deluxe hardcover & box set version a printing cost.

By joining our movement to rebuild the modern Library of Alexandria, you become part of an unprecedented mission to offer:

- **Unlimited Audiobook & eBook Access to the Greatest Classics of All Time**

  Instantly explore thousands of legendary works, from Plato and Shakespeare to Jane Austen and Leo Tolstoy. All are instantly ready to read or listen to, giving you a complete literary universe at your fingertips.

- **Paperback & Deluxe Editions at Printing Costs:**

  Purchase any title in a paperback, deluxe hardbound, or deluxe boxset edition at printing costs, shipped right to your doorstep. Curate your personal library of Alexandria with editions worthy of display—crafted to last, designed to captivate, and delivered straight to your door.

- **Modern translations for Contemporary Readers in all languages and dialects**

Discover a vast selection of classics reimagined in clear, current language—no more struggling with outdated phrases or obscure references. Next to the original versions, we aim to offer translations in as many languages and dialects as possible.

As we continue our translation efforts and add new languages, readers everywhere can connect with these works as if they were written today. By bridging linguistic divides, you're contributing to ensuring that these timeless stories become more meaningful, accessible, and inspiring for people across the globe.

- **Your Personal Library of Alexandria:**

Over the months and years, you'll curate a unique physical archive of classics—each volume a testament to your taste, curiosity, and love of knowledge. It's not just about owning books—it's about curating a cultural legacy you'll cherish and pass down for generations to come.

- **Join a Global Literary Renaissance:**

Your support fuels an ongoing mission: allowing us to reinvest in offering deluxe print editions (including special boxsets) at their true cost, broaden the range of available formats and translations, and extend the reach of these works to new audiences worldwide. By joining today, you're not just preserving a legacy of masterpieces; you set in motion a powerful wave of literary accessibility.

We are more than a publisher—we're a movement, and we can't do it alone. Your support lets us scale our mission, preserving and reimagining history's greatest works for tomorrow's readers.

Become a Torchbearer of knowledge.

Thank you for picking up this book and allowing us into your literary journey. As you turn the pages, know that you're part of something larger: a global effort to keep these stories alive, share their wisdom across borders and generations, and spark a true cultural revival for the modern era.

If this resonates with you—please consider taking the next step by visiting:

www.libraryofalexandria.com

With gratitude and a shared love of knowledge,

The Modern Library of Alexandria Team

Visit:

www.libraryofalexandria.com

Or scan the code below: